MW01171891

פניני חיים

פנינים לפרשת השבוע ולמועדים

ע"פ הדרשות של מו"ר **הרב אליהו בן-חיים** שליט"א

INSIGHTS ON THE WEEKLY PARASHA
AND THE JEWISH HOLIDAYS

Based on the teachings of

Harav Eliyahu Ben-Haim

First Edition

By: Rabbi Mosheh Aziz and Rabbi Chaim Levtov

Penine Ḥaim: Insights on the Weekly Parasha and the Jewish Holidays Based on the teachings of Harav Eliyahu Ben-Haim

This book contains many Jewish ideas. We have done our best to record them accurately and to provide sources for the subject matter. We are open to hearing comments and observations, particularly from rabbis and *talmide ḥachamim*, so that we can improve on our work for future editions.

Please address all communications to:

Sephardic Bet Midrash
695 Middle Neck Rd.
Great Neck, NY 11024

RabbiMosheh.Aziz@gmail.com

chaim.levtov@gmail.com

First Edition, 2024: ISBN 9798327126794 (Hardcover)

Printed in the United States of America

In Loving Memory of

ABDULRAHIM
EPHRAIM LEVIAN Z"L
אפרים בן משה ז"ל
1 ADAR 1 5760

RAFAEL ETESSAMI Z"L
רפאל בן הרצל יונתן ז"ל
13 TAMMUZ 5778

Dedicated by
Mrs. Pary Levian & Family

In Loving Memory of

ABDOULHAMID AGHALARIAN Z"L
שמעון בן יוסף ז"ל
21 NISSAN 5746

MOLOOK AGHALARIAN Z"L
מלכה בת אלעזר ז"ל
26 TEVET 5779

Dedicated by Aghalarian Family

In Loving Memory of

SAMI HAJIBAY Z"L
שמואל בן אברהם ז"ל
10 AV, 5777

Dedicated by

Miriam Hajibay & Family

In Loving Memory of

FARHAD HAKIMIAN z"l
יעקב בן משה ז"ל
22 ADAR II 5782

Dedicated by
Mrs. Mahyar Hakimian and Family

In Loving Memory of

HAROUN KOHANIM z"l
אהרן בן משיח ז"ל
16 TEVET 5762

FEREYDOUN RAHMANAN z"l
ראובן בן עמנואל ז"ל
12 IYYAR 5782

KHOSROW & MANIJEH HAKIM z"l
יעקב בן בנימין ז"ל
23 TAMMUZ 5782
מרים בת יהודה ז"ל
10 KISLEV 5779

Dedicated by Natascha and Aaron Kohanim

Dedicated by Ryan & Pamela Zar

in honor of their children

BELLA & MIA

We would also like to thank the following individuals for their contributions in supporting our work:

Anonymous

Anonymous
In Honor of his אשת חיל and their children

Levi Afrah
For Refuah Shelemah of Aliza Raizel Bracha Bat Yehudit Chava,
בתוך שאר חולי ישראל

Adam Aziz

Morris and Rika Aziz

Rabbi Mosheh Aziz

Solomon Bassalian

Rabbi Dr. Avraham Ben-Haim

Joshua and Adina Behar

Roey Kohanim

Rabbi Meyer Laniado

David Yisrael Levian
For the health of Rav Ben-Haim and his continued impact on our community

Rabbi Chaim Levtov

Naomi and Rabbi Michael Livi
In honor of their son Daniel

Chayim Mahgerefteh, CPA

Isaac Ovadia

Isaac Sachmechi

Aharon Zarnighian

בס"ד
הועד לעניני הדת
RELIGIOUS COUNCIL
United Mashadi Jewish Community of America

בס"ד
אייר תשפ"ד
May 2024

Rabbi Eliyahu Ben-Haim
(Co-Chair)

Mr. Nissim Bassalian
(Co-Chair)

Mr. Robert Livi
(Secretary)

Rabbi Mardechay Kahanim
Rabbi Yosef Bitton
Rabbi Adam Sabzevari
Rabbi Mosheh Aziz

Mr. Shmuel Livian
Mr. Louis Ebrani
Mr. Morris Aziz
Mr. Mehrdad Kahanim
Mr. Doron Hakimian
Mr. Besalel Ben-Haim
Mr. Moshe Enayatian
Mr. Adam Kordvani
Mr. Joshua Levian

The Religious Council was presented with the Sefer Penine Haim, authored by our own Rabbi Mosheh Aziz and by Rabbi Chaim Levtov. We reviewed the sefer in its entirety and are proud to endorse it.

We are fortunate to have a publication that preserves the Divre Torah of our esteemed Rav, מורנו הרב הגאון רבי אליהו בן חיים שליט"א. The Divre Torah were diligently transcribed and wonderfully present the Torah that Harav Ben-Haim has shared during his many years as the Rav and chief halachic authority of our community.

The Religious Council approves and endorses this publication. We thank Rabbi Aziz and Rabbi Levtov for their hard work in preparing the book. We hope that its messages and lessons will inspire all of Am Yisrael on a weekly basis with Harav Ben-Haim's pearls of wisdom on the parasha and the Jewish holidays.

With blessings,

UMJCA Religious Council

Rabbinical Court		בית דין צדק
New York		ניו יורק

147-02 76th Road Flushing NY 11367   347-415-5681

Rabbi Eliyahu Ben-Chaim, Chairman

בס"ד

כח' אייר יום ירושלים תשפ"ד
מג' למטמונים

<u>הסכמה</u>

שמחתי ויגל לבי על העבודה הנפלאה שעשו שנים מיקירי הרבנים שכתבו
את הדרשות שערכתי והם הרבנים הגאונים הרב חיים לב טוב והרב משה
הכהן עזיז. את הכל עשו יפה, דבר דבור על אפניו, יישר חילם. בטוחני
שדבריהם יעשו פירות, ואני תקוה שהדברים שכתבו ישפיעו על רבים.
הרב משה כתב כמה ספרים חשובים בהלכות נדה ובהלכות צדקה
ובהלכות שמחות, עליו אני אומר אם חכם לבך ישמח לבי גם אני. חזקו
ואמצו.

נאם : הרב אליהו בן חיים

TABLE OF CONTENTS

Table of Contents

Penine Ḥaim

PREFACE

First and foremost, we must express our infinite gratitude to Hashem, Master of the Universe, Who has carried us to this day and allowed the project of compiling this *Sefer* to become a reality.

The weekly parasha is a foundational element of every Jewish home and community. As Jews, we grow up with the expectation of learning and knowing the parasha on a weekly basis. We read the parasha Shenayim Mikra Ve'ehad Targum, and the parasha is read in synagogue from the Sefer Torah on a weekly basis. Rabbis commonly give their weekly derashot based on the parasha, and Divre Torah on the parasha are commonly shared at every Shabbat table.

Our Rav, Harav Eliyahu Ben-Haim, regularly shares short ideas on the parasha at the end of his shiurim throughout the week. He has shared these ideas with us during the years he taught in the Yeshiva University Sephardic Bet Midrash as well as in shiurim he continues to deliver at the Sephardic Bet Midrash Kollel in Great Neck, and in the Mashadi Jewish community where he serves as Chief Rabbi. (The collections of many parasha derashot, along with many other derashot from Rav Ben-Haim are recorded and can be accessed at YUTorah.org and www.youtube.com on the Rav Ben-Haim הרב אליהו בן-חיים channel.)

Over the years, we have noticed that Rav Ben-Haim does not hesitate to repeat some of his derashot on many of the parashiyot; in fact, it has always been critical importance that many of these messages be repeated on a regular basis so that the Torah's timeless values will be ingrained in our Jewish communities. With this in mind, we saw it as an important contribution to begin transcribing Rav Ben-Haim's derashot into English, to make them accessible to the English-reading public.

This book has undergone many drafts and is a product of approximately 24 months of work. Since June 2022, Rabbi Chaim Levtov, a long-time student of Rav Ben-Haim, has transcribed one Devar Torah every week from our audio recordings. The recorded Divre Torah were all delivered in Hebrew and were translated into English. In addition to transcribing the recordings, Rabbi Levtov also looked up and documented the sources that Rav Ben-Haim quoted so that the reader can easily access them. On a weekly basis, since December 2022, the transcribed Divre Torah have been published by Sephardic Bet Midrash in our Penine Haim newsletter, which is distributed in the Mashadi synagogues in Great Neck. Our vision from the start was to collect all the transcribed Divre Torah at the end of the year and publish this *Sefer* upon completing the one-year cycle. Additionally, we collected Rav Ben-Haim's Divre Torah for the various Jewish holidays throughout the year. We would like to thank the Mikrae Kodesh team, especially Shawn Aziz and Daniel Dilamani, for sharing their archives with us and some of Rav Ben-Haim's previously transcribed Divre Torah for the Jewish holidays.

After the one-year cycle was finished, considerable time was spent reviewing and editing the materials carefully with Rabbi Mosheh Aziz as the chief editor. We hope that the final product is found to be concise, clear, and organized. The sources that are quoted can be found in the footnotes at the end bottom of each page.

There may be slight stylistic changes in how we transcribed and edited Rav Ben-Haim's Divre Torah. We did our very best not to veer from Rav Ben-Haim's primary message in each Devar Torah. We hope that we did not make errors in transcribing or editing Rav Ben-Haim's Divre Torah. If any reader of the book has any comments or corrections, please reach out to us so that we can correct the book for the next edition.

Our heartfelt gratitude goes to the many talented individuals who generously gave their time and assisted us along the journey towards bringing this project to its final version. In particular, we would like to thank Rav Ben-Haim's grandsons, Eliyahu and Yehuda BenChaim, for carefully reviewing the entire manuscript and sharing their comments. We would also like to thank Mrs. Kelley Nitzani for proofreading the manuscript and sharing her comments. Their proofreading and valuable input contributed tremendously to the quality and clarity of this book.

We would like to acknowledge and thank Morenu Verabenu Nassim Bassalian, Rabbi Mordechay Kohanim, Rabbi Yosef Bitton, Rabbi Adam Sabzevari, Robert Livi, Doron Hakimian, Louis Ebrani, Shmuel Livian, Morris Aziz (father of Rabbi Mosheh Aziz), Mehrdad Kohanim, Moshe Enayatian, Besalel BenHaim, Adam Kordvani of the UMJCA Religious Council for their continued support, and for reviewing the manuscript and approving it for our community.

We would like to especially thank Josh Levian and Sephardic Bet Midrash for supporting our work as well as all the donors who made the publication of this book possible.

It is our prayer that this book should serve to assist rabbis and speakers with short ideas that they can use for their derashot (or parts of derashot) on Shabbat and Chagim, as well as inspire Jewish families with a short idea on the weekly parasha every week that can enrich the Shabbat table.

Rabbi Mosheh Aziz
Rabbi Chaim Levtov
Iyyar 5784

Penine Ḥaim

BERESHIT

2

Penine Ḥaim

פרשת בראשית

Parashat Bereshit

Erasing Jealousy

וַיֹּאמֶר קַיִן אֶל הֶבֶל אָחִיו וַיְהִי בִּהְיוֹתָם בַּשָּׂדֶה וַיָּקָם קַיִן אֶל הֶבֶל אָחִיו
וַיַּהַרְגֵהוּ:

"And Kayin spoke to Hevel, his brother, and it came to pass when they were in the field, that Kayin rose up against Hevel, his brother, and slew him."[1]

Pause for a moment and contemplate: Kayin and Hevel, the two sons of Adam, both had so much. The entire world could have been split in half for them: half for Kayin and half for Hevel. Both could have everything they could have ever desired. Should there have been any room for one to be jealous of the other? The entire world was available for just the two of them. However great their fortune, Kayin ultimately came to murder his younger brother Hevel. How could it be that Kayin came to murder his brother Hevel in cold blood? The answer lies in one word: jealousy. The sense of sibling

---

[1] Bereshit 4:8

rivalry that Kayin felt towards Hevel is the first example of jealousy in human history.

Jealousy is one of the gravest shortcomings of mankind. Pirke Avot[2] teaches us that jealousy removes a person from this world. In other words, jealousy distorts a person's perception; it causes a person to say things and engage in behaviors he or she could never have imagined taking part in. In this first instance of jealousy, it caused a brother who had all the blessings one could ever have in the world to ruthlessly murder his younger brother in cold blood.

The Gemara[3] quotes the verse in Mishle[4]: "The rotting of bones is caused by envy." The Gemara then expounds upon this verse to teach that when one possesses envy during his lifetime, his bones will rot inside him until his death; on the other hand, one who does not have any envy during his lifetime will not have his bones rot, even after he passes away. A famous story is told about the great Rav Abdallah Somech (19th century CE), the rabbi of the Jews of Baghdad and the author of Zivḥe Tzedek.[5] Rav Somech passed away during a cholera epidemic, and at the time, his body was not able to be buried in the Jewish cemetery in Iraq. After months of lobbying by the Jewish community, permission was granted to move his body to be buried in the Jewish cemetery. Shockingly, his body was found to be completely intact. It had not fallen into decay, even several months later. The great rabbis at the time attested that Rav Abdallah Somech truly did not harbor any envy in his heart; even when his student Rav Yosef Ḥaim (the Ben Ish Ḥai) gained fame during his lifetime, Rav Abdallah Somech still attended his student's classes

---

[2] Pirke Avot 4:21
[3] Shabbat 152b
[4] Mishle 14:30
[5] The story can be found in the introduction to the author's most famous work, Zivḥe Tzedek.

with humility. It was Rav Abdallah Somech's humility and lack of envy that allowed his body to be saved from any decay even after several months.

One of our most important tasks in life is to learn how to remove jealousy from our hearts and consequently, educate our children not to be jealous as well. A common cause for envy developing in a family is due to parents showing favoritism towards certain family members. Parents must never show favoritism towards any specific child, in order that children do not come to be jealous of each other. The Gemara[6] teaches that Yaakov Avinu made the mistake of showing favoritism towards Yosef over his other children. Due to the wool tunic that Yaakov gave to Yosef, jealousy arose in the family, and our forefathers were forced into being exiled to Egypt. Based on this, the Gemara teaches that one should never show favoritism to one child in one's home. The catalyst for our forefathers being sent to exile for hundreds of years was this one instance of favoritism that Yaakov displayed to Yosef.

To reduce jealousy, we always must count the blessings that we have and be appreciative of them. We must educate our children from a young age to recognize the blessings that they have from Hashem and to be content with those blessings. As a result of feeling content and blessed with their own lives, they hopefully will not feel the need to scrutinize the lives and possessions of those around them. When we erase jealousy from our hearts, we will be able to attain harmony in our relationships with our spouses, families, friends, and communities.

---

[6] Shabbat 10b, and Bereshit Rabba 84:8

פרשת נח

Parashat Noaḥ

The Art of Praise

וַיֹּאמֶר ה׳ לְנֹחַ בֹּא אַתָּה וְכָל בֵּיתְךָ אֶל הַתֵּבָה כִּי אֹתְךָ רָאִיתִי צַדִּיק לְפָנַי בַּדּוֹר
הַזֶּה:

*"Hashem said to Noaḥ, 'Come to the Ark, you and your family. For
I have seen you as righteous before me in this generation.'"* [7]

The Torah is known for extreme precision in its word choice. We
see this precision in how Noaḥ is described in our parasha. At the
beginning of our Parasha, the first verse that describes Noaḥ says:
"Noaḥ was a righteous man, perfect in his generation; Noaḥ walked
with Hashem." We see a comprehensive description of Noaḥ's
righteousness: he was righteous, and he was perfect and walked with
Hashem. In the second verse, quoted above, Hashem says said to
Noaḥ: "I have seen you as a righteous person before me in this
generation." Here, Hashem simply calls Noaḥ "righteous." Why the
difference?

---

[7] Bereshit 7:1

The Gemara,[8] cited by Rashi, answers that the Torah here teaches us a lesson in proper etiquette: excessive praise in someone's presence is inappropriate. Noaḥ was the same righteous man from the beginning of the parasha up until this point. The first verse offers a general description of Noaḥ, which allows a complete description of his great character. In the second verse, however, Hashem is speaking directly to Noaḥ himself. It is considered improper to offer a person's complete praise in front of him. Therefore, the Torah limits itself to describing him as just "righteous." This teaches us a valuable lesson about both the power and pitfalls of praise. Rashi[9] explains that we must be mindful to avoid excessive flattery in a person's presence, since it can be interpreted as insincere or manipulative. Genuine appreciation can hold much more weight when it is delivered in a person's absence as opposed to in their presence.

Unfortunately, it is common to see that some individuals act exactly in the opposite manner from this example in the Torah. When they are in the presence of a person, they will shower them with exaggerated compliments, as if they are their greatest friend and supporter. However, when the person is absent, they will stab them in the back and speak negatively about them. Such behavior goes directly against the ethical principles of the Torah. The Gemara[10] teaches in the name of the great sage Hillel: "That which you would not like, do not do to others. This is the entire Torah; the rest is commentary." Certainly, no person would like for others to speak negatively behind their back. Therefore, we should not engage in such behavior either.

---

[8] Eruvin 18b, quoted by Rashi Bereshit 7:1
[9] Eruvin 18b
[10] Shabbat 31b

By following the Gemara's principle and avoiding excessive praise, we can build stronger and more genuine relationships. If we speak a certain way in a person's presence, it should only be that we would speak even better of them in the case of their absence. This will foster greater harmony and respect in our communities, thus following the sacred guidelines of the Torah for how we build our relationships.

פרשת לך לך

Parashat Lech Lecha

There is Always a Plan

וַיֹּאמֶר ה׳ אֶל אַבְרָם לֶךְ לְךָ מֵאַרְצְךָ וּמִמּוֹלַדְתְּךָ וּמִבֵּית אָבִיךָ אֶל הָאָרֶץ אֲשֶׁר
אַרְאֶךָּ:

"Hashem said to Avraham, 'Go forth from your native land and from your father's house to the land that I will show you.'"[11]

As we read the stories of the book of Bereshit, we must remember that the stories recorded in the Torah are not only mentioned to record simple historical events. The Torah is not just a history book. As the Zohar[12] says, the stories in the Torah are also written to impart important values and messages for all generations.

In this week's Torah portion, Avraham and Sarah follow Hashem's instruction to leave their homeland to journey to the land of Canaan. Rashi[13] explains that three negative hardships befall a person who migrates from one place to another. Firstly, traveling makes it more

---

[11] Bereshit 12:1
[12] Behaalotecha 152a
[13] Bereshit 12:2

difficult to have and then children and raise children in the new location. Secondly, traveling affects a person's income by making it more difficult to earn a livelihood. Thirdly, traveling diminishes a person's name, since he must rebuild his reputation in a new place. Avraham Avinu felt all three of these natural worries of moving to a new place. How would he make a living? How would he be able to have children? How would he build a reputation for himself if no one knew him? To address all three of these concerns, Hashem reassured him by promising Avraham that he would have many descendants, he would be blessed with wealth, and his name would become great.

The struggle that Avraham faced is relevant to all of us in our respective journeys in life. Many times, a person faces a situation that seems negative, but in the long term it turns out to be only for the person's good. To illustrate, the Gemara[14] tells a story of two people who left their homes to go on a business trip on a boat. On the way to the boat, one of them stepped on a thorn and injured his foot, and he was consequently unable to travel on the boat with his colleague. He started blaspheming and cursing in frustration that he was unable to travel. After a short period of time, he heard that the boat that his friend traveled on had capsized at sea. He only realized then that the thorn he stepped on had saved his life from a very certain death. The man then started thanking God and praising Him for his salvation due to the slight pain caused to him by the thorn.

We must always do our best to internalize the fact that what we see in front of us in life is not always the full picture. Often, we might think a situation appears to be terrible, only to realize later that it was only for our benefit.

---

[14] Nidda 31a

Rav Ben-Haim would often mention how he would vividly remember people crying and so depressed when leaving Iran. They thought they would be poor and alone in the United States. However, so many of the same Jews became financially successful and were able to raise their children in the ways of Torah only due to the fact they came to America. The history of the State of Israel was the same. When the Israeli War of Independence broke out in 1948, there was famine and great suffering across the country. Many lost hope and thought this would be the end of the Jewish people. No one could imagine how Israel began to flourish as a country in such a short period of time. The lesson for us is that in challenging times, we should never despair or lose hope. We must remember and internalize that Hashem runs the world and has a plan for us, which is ultimately only for our benefit, even if sometimes we might not immediately see the big picture.

פרשת וירא

Parashat Vayera

The Legacy of Avraham: Bringing People Closer

וַיֵּרָא אֵלָיו ה' בְּאֵלֹנֵי מַמְרֵא וְהוּא יֹשֵׁב פֶּתַח הָאֹהֶל כְּחֹם הַיּוֹם:

"Hashem appeared to him by the plains of Mamre; he was sitting at the entrance of the tent in the heat of the day."[15]

Our parasha tells a powerful story of Avraham Avinu's immense kindness. The Gemara[16] explains that this day was no ordinary day for Avraham. It was the third day after his Berit Milah, which was the most painful day of recovery from the surgery. Even as an old man, and physically weak from a surgery, Avraham sat by the opening of his tent, looking for guests to welcome into his home. Upon seeing three strangers pass by, Avraham did not just invite them in, but he ran to greet them with the enthusiasm of a young man. Further highlighting how impressive Avraham's kindness was, Rashi[17] notes that Avraham Avinu suspected these men could be

---

[15] Bereshit 18:1
[16] Bava Metzia 86b
[17] Rashi Bereshit 18:4

idol worshippers, possibly part of an Arab cult that worships that dirt on their feet. Therefore, he asked the strangers to wash their feet before entering his home, to ensure that no idols would be brought into his home. Yet, even with such suspicions, Avraham eagerly extended his hospitality to these potentially wicked individuals. Only later did Avraham learn that these men were angels and not idolaters.

We learn a tremendous lesson from Avraham. Regardless of whether we perceive someone as distant from Judaism, we should never lose faith in their potential. Even though he was elderly and in pain, Avraham Avinu strengthened himself with his last few energies to prioritize kindness over his own needs. We should always strive to see the positive potential within every person, regardless of the external factors. This way, we can work passionately, as Avraham Avinu did, to bring unaffiliated Jews closer to Hashem.

Rav Ovadia Yosef z"l, the former chief Sephardic rabbi of Israel, would commonly quote an inspiring legend. The legend says that one time, Avraham Avinu once hosted a 90-year old man for a meal. At the end of the meal, Avraham Avinu asked the man to say Birkat Hamazon and thank Hashem for his food.[18] The man responded by pulling his personal idol out of his pocket and kissing it. Avraham proceeded to debate the man for several hours, trying to convince him of the existence of Hashem and futility of idol worship. After six hours, Avraham was unsuccessful, and the stubborn idol worshipper refused to leave his idol worship. Avraham Avinu grew impatient, and angrily dismissed him from the store. Immediately, Hashem appeared to Avraham and rebuked him, "Avraham, I patiently waited 90 years for this man to come back to Me, you

---

[18] Sota 10b

couldn't wait for him even a few hours?" Avraham then went and pursued the man, inviting him back to his tent for another meal. At the next meal, with love, kindness, and patience, Avraham persuaded the man back to belief in Hashem.

These stories emphasize the importance of "Kiruv," bringing others closer to Judaism with kindness, patience, and compassion. Every Jew has a spiritual spark inside them that can ignite their passion at any moment to come closer to Hashem. If we view every person with great positivity and potential, we can nurture the spiritual sparks within them to bring them closer to Hashem and our Torah. These stories of Avraham Avinu teach us to have unwavering faith in the positive potential of others.

פרשת חיי שרה

Parashat Ḥayye Sara

The Qualities of a Good Spouse

כִּי אֶל אַרְצִי וְאֶל מוֹלַדְתִּי תֵּלֵךְ וְלָקַחְתָּ אִשָּׁה לִבְנִי לְיִצְחָק:

"But go to the land of my birth and get a wife for my son Yitzḥak."[19]

This week's Parasha describes Avraham's quest to find a suitable spouse for Yitzḥak. Avraham designates his servant Eliezer to find this special wife for his son. Avraham instructs Eliezer to swear to him that he will not take a wife from the people of Canaan, rather, she should be from his homeland - the land of Ḥaran. Avraham insisted that Eliezer could only find a wife from his distant homeland and not from the area of Canaan where they were both found at that time. Why was Avraham so insistent on only taking a woman from Ḥaran and not from Canaan, and why did he insist on having Eliezer swear to him in such a unique way that he would follow his command?

---

[19] Bereshit 24:4

Rabbenu Nissim of Gerona (usually known by the acronym the "Ran")[20] explains that Avraham realized that Ḥaran was a pagan city whose inhabitants were deeply steeped in idolatry. It was Avraham's own homeland and he lived there for many years. At the same time, Avraham also knew that the people there were kind and well-mannered individuals with good character qualities. Although they were steeped in pagan practices, Avraham figured that these mistaken intellectual ideologies can easily be corrected with good education and Torah study. On the other hand, the people of Canaan were not kind or sensitive people. The culture of Canaan was not one that promoted kindness, and he knew that bad character qualities cannot be easily changed, even with many years of education. Therefore, Avraham did not want a wife for Yitzḥak from such a place; since character qualities cannot not easily be changed, it was of primary importance for his son to marry a girl with good character qualities. Avraham preferred a wife from the idolatrous, yet well-manner Ḥaran over the ill-mannered Canaan, since Avraham knew that it is easier to correct false theological ideologies than to correct bad character deficiencies. Finding a young woman with good character was the most important factor for finding a wife for his son Yitzḥak and Avraham knew that everything else would follow. We learn a tremendous lesson from this command of Avraham. When searching for a life partner, the most important factor that should be non-negotiable is *middot* - good character qualities. Good character is the most important recipe for a successful marriage. This factor was so important to Avraham that he was willing to search for such a woman for his son from a society that was not ideologically aligned with his own, with the expectation and knowledge that she will be later educated in Torah and mitzvot.

---

[20] Derashot Haran Derush #5

Good character traits are one of the only qualities of a spouse which can endure even after many years of marriage. External looks can be deceiving and always fade after time. As Shelomo Hamelech teaches us in Mishle:[21] "Like a gold ring in the snout of a pig is a beautiful woman bereft of judgement." External beauty without internal beauty has no value. But the good character qualities of a spouse are everlasting. When searching for a spouse, one must never lose focus of the most important qualities in a lifelong partner. External factors only have value when they accompany deep internal values. Avraham's conditions made it very clear that good character was the top priority, even higher than other important qualities. Avraham also realized that good character does not come by easily and is the most important quality for a happy marriage. When we constantly work on our character in marriage, we are investing in an everlasting bond in our relationships, which will only continue to flourish with health and happiness for many years to come, Amen.

---

[21] Mishle 11:12

פרשת תולדות

Parashat Toledot

Beyond Honesty: Communication with Sensitivity

וַיֶּאֱהַב יִצְחָק אֶת עֵשָׂו כִּי צַיִד בְּפִיו וְרִבְקָה אֹהֶבֶת אֶת יַעֲקֹב:

"Yitzḥak favored Esav because he had a taste for the game [that Esav brought] was in his mouth, but Rivka favored Yaakov."[22]

In Parashat Toledot, we are introduced to the story between our forefather Yaakov and his older brother Esav. The Parasha notes that Yitzḥak planned to give the main beracha to Esav, his wicked son, instead of giving the beracha to his righteous son Yaakov. Realizing what was going to happen, Rivka asked Yaakov to dress up as his brother, Esav, to deceive his father and steal the berachot that Esav was meant to receive. An obvious question can be asked: why did Rivka have to go behind the back of her husband and sneak the berachot away from Esav? Why did she not approach her husband and tell Yitzḥak directly that he was making a mistake by giving the blessing to the wicked Esav instead of giving it to Yaakov?

---

[22] Bereshit 25:28

In fact, we learn a tremendous lesson here about how careful one must be with speaking negatively about others, particularly in the context of marriage. Even though Yaakov was truly destined to receive the beracha from his father, Rivka was extremely cautious about pointing out her husband's misjudgment regarding his approach to Esav. Rivka did not want to hurt Yitzḥak by revealing Esav's negative nature to him and that he was mistaken in his perception. Although it would have been the truth, Rivka felt that this would be a slight towards her husband's honor and understanding, and therefore, refrained from confronting him directly. The lesson to be learned from this is how careful we must be when speaking about others, especially when speaking to one's spouse.

We find that Rivka continued to act with this approach at the end of the Parasha as well. When Yaakov received the blessing and she found out that Esav wanted to kill him, Rivka did not tell her husband that their son Esav wanted to murder his brother Yaakov. Instead, she told her husband that it is time for Yaakov to get married, and that Yaakov must travel to her homeland to find a wife. This way, he could go find a wife and save himself from Esav at the same time, and Yitzḥak would not be pained to find out that Esav wants to murder Yaakov. We see again how sensitive Rivka was about not allowing her husband to be hurt. She worked diligently to avoid her husband going through the pain of hearing he has a son who is wicked, while still working to ensure that Yaakov would receive the blessing.

There is a halacha that is reminiscent of this concept. Shulḥan Aruch[23] writes in the laws of mourning that according to the letter of the law, we do not have to tell a person that his relative passed

---

[23] Shulḥan Aruch Yoreh Deah 402:12

away if he does not know about it yet. It is not necessary to put a person in that kind of pain. Nowadays, we generally do mention the news of a person passing to allow the relatives to perform the mitzvah of burying their relative and saying Kaddish for him. However, for example, if a person is sick in the hospital and their relative passes away, we would not inform them that the relative passed away, since telling them would only cause them unnecessary pain. At any rate, we see from here how sensitive we must be to not cause any unnecessary pain when speaking to others and that we must always be sensitive in protecting every person's honor and feelings to the extent possible.

פרשת ויצא

Parashat Vayetze

Understanding Yaakov's Prayer

וַיִּדַּר יַעֲקֹב נֶדֶר לֵאמֹר אִם יִהְיֶה אֱ-לֹהִים עִמָּדִי וּשְׁמָרַנִי בַּדֶּרֶךְ הַזֶּה אֲשֶׁר אָנֹכִי הוֹלֵךְ וְנָתַן לִי לֶחֶם לֶאֱכֹל וּבֶגֶד לִלְבֹּשׁ : וְשַׁבְתִּי בְשָׁלוֹם אֶל בֵּית אָבִי וְהָיָה ה' לִי לֵא-לֹהִים :

"Yaakov then made a vow, saying, "If[24] Hashem remains with me, protecting me on this journey that I am making, and giving me bread to eat, and clothing to wear. And I return safe to my father's house - Hashem shall be my God."[25]

At the beginning of this week's Parasha, Yaakov is running away from his brother Esav. Yaakov declares to Hashem: "*If* Hashem will be with me, protecting me and taking care of my needs on this journey, then Hashem will be my God." Yaakov's declaration raises an immediate concern. What does his condition mean? Does Yaakov

---

[24] Or "When", as will be explained.
[25] Bereshit 29:21-22

mean to say that he will only accept Hashem as his God if Hashem protects him and takes care of his needs? What if, *ḥas veshalom*, Hashem would not do so? Would Hashem no longer be Yaakov's God if He wouldn't do as Yaakov had requested? How can one ever make such a condition with Hashem?

The answer is that, of course, a Jew's faith in Hashem cannot be dependent on how Hashem seems to act towards us. Even amongst hardships, Hashem is our Father. Rav Ben-Haim once read that a letter was found in the Warsaw Ghetto during the Holocaust that read: "Hashem, with all the suffering we are experiencing, do you also want us to deny Your existence? You will not succeed. Even amongst all the pain we experience, we will always trust You and have faith in You." One of the most famous examples of unconditional faith in Hashem was the famous Rebbe of Klausenburg, Rav Yekutiel Yehudah Halberstam. The saintly rabbi's entire family was slaughtered by the Nazis in the Holocaust: his wife, ten children, his mother, and his brothers and sisters. His oldest son initially survived the war but died soon after in a refugee camp. Nonetheless, the rabbi never lost his faith in Hashem. He made an oath to Hashem that if he survives the war, he will build a hospital that will provide medical care to Jews and save Jewish lives. After the war, he fulfilled his oath and established the Laniado hospital in Netanya, Israel, amongst many other great accomplishments in his life.

Yaakov Avinu was our great forefather, and certainly his faith in Hashem was no less. How could it be, therefore, that Yaakov Avinu bases his faith in Hashem on the condition of good health and a livelihood? The answer is that Yaakov did not actually make such a conditional statement. We find that Rashi[26] points out that in several

---

[26] Shemot 22:24 and other places

places in the Torah, the word אם can carry different connotations. For example, sometimes it means "if" while other times it must be translated as "when". Yaakov's declaration of אם was not Yaakov making a condition with Hashem. Rather Yaakov was saying: "Hashem, it will be <u>when</u> you take care of me and my needs, and protect me on this path, then I will be able to serve you better as my God." In other words, Yaakov understood that if he did not have his basic life necessities taken care of, such as livelihood and good health, it would be much more difficult to serve Hashem properly. Therefore, he was praying to Hashem to be granted protection so that his needs would be taken care of, and then. he could serve Hashem with proper focus.

We find that Rambam[27] shares the true explanation of the concepts of blessings and rewards that we read every day in Shema Yisrael. The verses of Shema describe that when we listen to the words of Hashem in the Torah, Hashem will grant us rain in its proper times, as well as an abundance of wealth and produce. Could it be that the reward for keeping mitzvot are only the material rewards of having rain in its proper time and to have successful businesses? Of course not! As the Gemara[28] famously teaches, rewards for the mitzvot that we do are not granted in this world, rather, they are granted in the World to Come! Truly, the verses of Shema can be explained in accordance with what we explained about Yaakov Avinu - the material blessings granted to us in this world are not granted as an end in and of themselves. Rather, they are given to enable us to continue to serve Hashem in the best way, so that we can further earn reward in the World to Come.

---

[27] Halachot Teshuva 9:1
[28] Kiddushin 39b

We must always stay steadfast in our faith in Hashem, even in times when things do not seem to go our way. Yaakov Avinu maintained this faith and was prepared to serve Hashem, whether Hashem would bless him or would not bless him. At the same time, we always ask Hashem to bless us with all our needs and therefore enable us to serve Him without restraint. This was the prayer of Yaakov Avinu in our Parasha, and the model for all our prayers as well.

פרשת וישלח

Parashat Vayishlaḥ

The Threat of Brotherhood

הַצִּילֵנִי נָא מִיַּד אָחִי מִיַּד עֵשָׂו כִּי יָרֵא אָנֹכִי אֹתוֹ פֶּן יָבוֹא וְהִכַּנִי אֵם עַל בָּנִים :

"Save me, I pray, from the hand of my brother, from the hand of Esav; for I fear him, lest he come and smite me, the mother with the children."[29]

This week's Parasha introduces the confrontation between Yaakov and Esav, many years after Yaakov had escaped from his brother who had wanted to kill him. Yaakov was anxious about the confrontation with Esav and his army of 400 men. As part of his preparations, Yaakov prays to Hashem to save him from his brother, Esav.

Many commentaries ask a famous question on this verse. We know that the Torah does not use any extra words when they are unnecessary. Yaakov appears to use redundant language in his prayer, asking to be saved "from the hand of my brother, from the

---

[29] Bereshit 32:12,

hand of Esav." On the surface, it would have been enough for him say either, "Save me from the hand of Esav," or, "Save me from the hand of my brother." Why does Yaakov Avinu use a seemingly unnecessary double language, asking to be saved both from his brother and from Esav?

At the start of the 19th century, there was a bloody war between the French and Russian empires. The famous emperor of the French, Napoleon Bonaparte, decided to invade Russia with his army. The Russians, at the time, were known to persecute the Jews terribly, while Napoleon was known to be more liberal in his policies and much more kind to the Jews. Most of European Jewry therefore prayed for the success of Napoleon and the downfall of the Russians. However, Rabbi Shneur Zalman of Liadi, the first Lubavitcher Rebbe, prayed for the success of the Russian Tsar and even assisted the Russians in the war. When asked about why he would pray for antisemites to succeed, Rabbi Shneur Zalman explained that in his opinion, the spiritual danger of a friendly government was a greater threat than the physical danger of an antisemitic one. Although Napoleon was accepting of Jews and would create an environment of religious tolerance, he was also committed to assimilating Jews into French society. This would eventually result in high assimilation rates and deterioration of Jewish values. Under religious persecution of antisemitic governments, most Jews would guard their Jewish values faithfully. With emancipation, however, the Jews would let go of their Judaism freely and willingly to attain higher recognition in French society. This insight from the Rabbi Schneur Zalman can shed light on Yaakov's concern when confronting Esav.

The Bet Halevi,[30] Rabbi Yosef Dov Soloveitchik, explains that when Yaakov prayed to Hashem to be saved from Esav, he was describing two different tactics Esav could have used to sabotage him. The first tactic was through the hateful "Esav," which represents antisemitic enemies such as Haman and Hitler, who mercilessly persecuted all Jews with their racist hatred. But, Yaakov also prayed to be saved from the other threat that Esav might have employed - "my brother." Esav could have also harmed Yaakov by pretending to befriend him and show him love, while internally planning to eradicate him of any spirituality and holiness. This tactic of "my brother" can sometimes be an even greater threat than the first, since a Jew might not even be aware of the dangers and compromise his Judaism of his own free will.

Unfortunately, when we consider the state of American Jewry today, Yaakov Avinu's concerns have never been more relevant. If we look at the world population of Jews since the time of the Holocaust, population statistics have shown that a "silent holocaust" of assimilation and intermarriage since the Holocaust has led to the loss and prevention of the birth of more Jews than the Holocaust itself. As Jews, we must worry just as much about the dangers of intermarriage as much as we must worry about antisemitism. Yaakov was keenly aware of the threat of both approaches of Esav, and therefore prayed to be saved from both of his tactics. In the merit of Jews marrying Jews and remaining true to our values, we should merit to see our Jewish population only grow.

---

[30] Bet Halevi Parashat Vayishlaḥ

פרשת וישב

Parashat Vayeshev

Divine Providence

וַיִּקְחוּ אֶת כְּתֹנֶת יוֹסֵף וַיִּשְׁחֲטוּ שְׂעִיר **עִזִּים** וַיִּטְבְּלוּ אֶת הַכֻּתֹּנֶת בַּדָּם:

*"Then they took Joseph's tunic, slaughtered **a goat,** and dipped the tunic in the blood."[31]*

One of the cornerstones of Judaism is our belief in Divine Providence. Hashem oversees all that occurs in the universe. Everything is orchestrated by Hashem for a specific purpose in a way that is precise and calculated, and nothing is overlooked. Hashem runs the world "*Midda Keneged Midda,*" or "measure for measure". Any act of kindness we perform or positive thought that we have is accounted for, and every hurtful or sinful action is accounted for by Hashem. An amazing example of Divine Providence can be seen in our Parasha.

In Parashat Toledot, our forefather Yaakov deceived his father and stole the blessings from his brother Esav. The Torah recounts that

---

[31] Bereshit 37:3

when Esav first went hunting to receive the blessing of the first born from their father, their mother Rivka hatched a plan for Yaakov to secure the blessing without Yitzhak knowing. The Torah states: "And she covered his hands and the hairless part of his neck <u>with the skins of the goats.</u>"[32] In other words, Rivka dressed Yaakov's hands and neck in goat fur, to make his father think he was Esav. Although Yaakov was following his mother's instructions and only had good intentions, at the end of the day, he deceived his father by dressing up as his older brother Esav. This deception, we find, eventually came back to hurt him in our Parasha.

In this week's Parasha, Yosef's ten older brothers abduct him and sell him as a slave to Egypt. To cover up their evil actions, they took Yosef's tunic and dipped it in <u>goat blood,</u> to make it appear that he was killed. The Midrash[33] notes the insertion of goats as part of the brothers' deception of their father Yaakov is not by accident. The Torah highlights that goats were used to deceive Yaakov to convey a deep message: the same way Yaakov deceived his father with the skins of goats, his sons deceived him many years later by slaughtering a goat. We see from here that there is no action that goes without consequence. Even though he may have had the best of intentions, Yaakov deceived his father. In the end, his own children deceived him in the same way.

This is a tremendous lesson for us to learn. Whatever we do will always come back to us. If we deceive others, someone else will eventually deceive us. If we steal from others, someone will steal from us. As the Gemara[34] teaches, "A person does not [even] stub his toe on this world unless it was decided so in Heaven." Every one

---

[32] Bereshit 27:16
[33] Ginze Schachter, quoted by Torah Shelema Bereshit 37:3
[34] Chulin 7b

of our actions is accounted for and measured to the smallest of amounts.

This lesson is true on the positive side as well: even the smallest mitzvah or act of kindness that we do is recognized by Hashem and we are rewarded for it. If we are generous and give to others, we will be repaid in kindness when we might be in need ourselves. When we do good, live righteously and with integrity, we can always rest assured that Hashem will reward us even for the smallest mitzvot and kindnesses that we perform.

פרשת מקץ

Parashat Miketz

Faith in the Future

וַתֹּאכַלְנָה הַפָּרוֹת רָעוֹת הַמַּרְאֶה וְדַקֹת הַבָּשָׂר אֵת שֶׁבַע הַפָּרוֹת יְפֹת הַמַּרְאֶה וְהַבְּרִיאֹת וַיִּיקַץ פַּרְעֹה:

"And the cows of ugly appearance and skinny of flesh devoured the seven cows that were of handsome appearance and healthy; then Pharaoh awoke."[35]

The year was 1978, it was when the revolution in Iran had already started. Exactly at this time of year, on this Shabbat of Parashat Miketz, Rav Ben-Haim vividly recalled the state of the Jewish community in Tehran. There were many protests and demonstrations already happening in the streets. The Jews of Iran were anxious about the revolution, which was potentially going to overthrow the Shah. There was an overwhelming sentiment of chaos, panic, and fear. Many had either left the country or were planning their escape from Iran. Rav Ben-Haim remembers Mr. Yousef Cohen, a Jewish member of the Iranian parliament, coming

---

[35] Bereshit 41:4

to synagogue on this exact Shabbat of Parashat Miketz and speaking to the Jewish community. In his speech, he gave the following message: "My dear friends, it pains me to tell you, the 'seven healthy cows' (i.e. the years of prosperity and blessing) for the Jews of Iran under the Shah have come to an end. The seven skinny cows are now going to begin." Most were crying and distressed over their personal future and over the bleak future of the Jewish community. The Iranian revolution would most certainly bring a negative outcome for the future of Iranian Jews.

Forty-five years later,[36] the Jews of our communities can say, in a broad and overall sense, the exact opposite came to be true. The Iranian Jewish community has grown and flourished since moving from Tehran to the United States. As one example, our own Mashadi Jewish community has, broadly speaking, experienced great blessing in America in every way, both in spiritual prosperity and in material prosperity. We now have greater attendance in our minyanim and knowledge of Torah than we ever had in Iran. More than ever, our youth attend our synagogues in large numbers, including many minyanim every morning [in Iran, Rav Ben-Haim noted, only the elderly would normally attend synagogue on a daily basis]. The homes that our community members live in here in the Unites States are, in general, much nicer than the homes in Tehran. The Mashadi community has even now established our own Mashadi yeshiva day school in Great Neck, MESA. All of this occurred, even though forty-five years ago, most members of the Jewish community of Iran were convinced that their future appeared hopeless. Hashem had much more blessing in store for us than we could have imagined.

---

[36] This Devar Torah was said by Rav Ben-Haim in 2023/5784.

The story of our community was also the story of Yosef and his brothers. Yosef was sold to slavery by his own brothers and put in jail for many years. He was expelled alone to a foreign land with nobody to support him. Without faith in Hashem, there was almost no possible way for Yosef to see those dark years as a slave to be beneficial in any way. But Hashem had other plans. It was only because Yosef was in prison at right time that Hashem orchestrated for him to become the viceroy of all of Egypt. Only because his brothers sold him as a slave to Egypt, Yosef became one of the most powerful men in the world and was able to support his family during the years of famine in Egypt. Yosef remained steadfast in his faith in Hashem throughout his entire time and remained optimistic throughout the difficult years in Egypt.

This is a tremendous lesson for all of us today. Many times, we face challenges that seem unexplainable to us and appear to be only to our detriment. We must believe that sometimes what seems bad in our eyes is only due to our limited perception of reality. Very often, the same life events that appear bad to us at first end up being only for the good. The Mishna[37] teaches us: "A person must say a blessing for the bad just as he says a blessing for the good." Hashem always has a plan for us which is ultimately for our benefit. May we be blessed to openly see Hashem's kindness in all aspects of our lives, Amen.

---

[37] Berachot 9:5

פרשת ויגש

Parashat Vayigash

The Courage to Forgive

וְעַתָּה אַל תֵּעָצְבוּ וְאַל יִחַר בְּעֵינֵיכֶם כִּי מְכַרְתֶּם אֹתִי הֵנָּה כִּי לְמִחְיָה שְׁלָחַנִי
אֱ-לֹהִים לִפְנֵיכֶם:

"Now, do not be distressed or reproach yourselves because you sold me here; it was to provide sustenance that Hashem sent me ahead of you."[38]

In the beginning of this week's Parasha, Yehuda confronts Yosef and delivers a passionate plea to Yosef to not take his youngest brother Binyamin as a prisoner. Yosef is overwhelmed with emotion from Yehuda's sincerity and finally reveals his identity to the brothers. Immediately upon revealing his identity, Yosef reassures his brothers, telling them not to be upset that they sold him to Egypt. The sale to Egypt was part of Hashem's Divine plan from the beginning. Yosef tells his brothers, "It was to provide sustenance that Hashem sent me here."

---

[38] Bereshit 45:5

Let us take an accounting. Yosef most certainly had every reason to bear a grudge against his brothers for the way they treated him when he was younger. His brothers had treated him as anything but a brother. They attempted to eliminate him from their family in the most merciless way. Now that Yosef was the viceroy of Egypt, the power was in his hands, and the opportunity for revenge was perfect. Yosef could have done anything he wanted to repay his brothers as they deserved for the trouble that they caused him when he was younger.

Amazingly, we find that Yosef did not do this. Instead of punishing them or taking revenge, Yosef tells the brothers not to be distressed or sorry that they sold him as a slave. With a clean and pure heart, Yosef had the incredible courage to let go of the past and open the door to start a new page with his brothers. He did not bear a grudge and completely forgave them for what had happened in the past. From Yosef, we learn the power of forgiving with a pure heart, to maintain peace amongst the Jewish people.

When we examine the stories of our forefathers in the Torah, we find that for several generations, every one of our forefathers failed to have all his sons unified in the ways of Hashem. Avraham had Yitzhak, but also had Yishmael. Yitzhak had Yaakov, but also had Esav. Yaakov had twelve sons who were already barreling down on the path once again towards eternal division and discord. If Yosef would have held his grudge against the brothers and had not forgiven them, the Jewish nation as we know it would certainly not exist today. The future of the entire Jewish nation as a whole was saved because of Yosef's tremendous courage in forgiving his brothers with a pure heart and seeing that everything in his life came from Hashem. Yosef never even told his father what his brothers did to him, just so that there would not be any extra friction in the household.

There are, unfortunately, many times where families fall into internal discord. Siblings are not willing to talk to each other for so many years, children and parents give each other silent treatment, and marriages fall apart for one reason or another. All these conflicts cause indescribable pain, as conflicts in the family only come to hurt everyone in the long term. Yosef teaches us the value of being able to let go of the past and having the courage to forgive, to pave the way for healing within a family.

The Gemara[39] tells of a time when there was a drought in Israel. Rabbi Eliezer ben Horkenos, the elder rabbi, prayed on behalf of the community, but his prayers were not answered. Then Rabbi Akiva, who was the younger rabbi at the time, prayed on behalf of the community. Rabbi Akiva's prayers were answered, and the rain fell. When the people saw this, they began to murmur against Rabbi Eliezer whose prayers were not answered. Then a voice came from Heaven and said, "It is not because Rabbi Akiva is a greater rabbi than Rabbi Eliezer that his prayers were answered; rather, Rabbi Akiva's prayers were answered because he is a forgiving person, whereas Rabbi Eliezer is not a forgiving person."

When we go out of our comfort zone to help forgive and maintain peace, we should hopefully see our prayers answered and see an overflow of blessings from Hashem.

---

[39] Taanit 25b

פרשת ויחי

Parashat Vayḥi

The Date of Mashiaḥ's Arrival

וַיְחִי יַעֲקֹב בְּאֶרֶץ מִצְרַיִם שְׁבַע עֶשְׂרֵה שָׁנָה וַיְהִי יְמֵי יַעֲקֹב שְׁנֵי חַיָּיו שֶׁבַע שָׁנִים
וְאַרְבָּעִים וּמְאַת שָׁנָה:

*"And Yaakov lived seventeen years in the land of Egypt; the total
number of years of Yaakov, the years of his living, were one hundred
forty-seven years."* [40]

When looking at the beginning of Parashat Vayḥi inside the Torah
scroll, one cannot help but notice that it is written in an unusual
manner. The Parasha does not start with the beginning of the
paragraph, the way every other Parasha in the Torah does. Rather,
Parashat Vayḥi starts with a verse that is right in the middle of a
paragraph, without any spacing, almost as a continuation of the
previous Parasha. Parashat Vayḥi stands unique as the only Parasha
in the Torah that starts in this way, right in the middle of a paragraph
and without a break in the page.

---

[40] Bereshit 47:28

Rashi[41] explains that this irregularity in the Torah alludes to a deeper point: Yaakov Avinu wanted to reveal to his children and grandchildren when the Jews will be redeemed and leave Egypt. However, Hashem "closed" his insight and did not allow it to be revealed to the Jewish people. Hashem did not want the Jewish people involving themselves with calculations of the future. The "closing" of space between the two parashiyot alludes to this episode with Yaakov and his sons.

This incident with Yaakov teaches us a profound lesson. Many times, people look for answers to life struggles by dissecting certain Torah texts and developing calculations based on numerical values of the Torah. They do so to determine future events such as when Mashiaḥ is going to come, or to find answers to explain why certain things happen to them in life. This is a very dangerous practice because it can lead people to believe in false ideas that were fabricated by their own imagination that are not actually truly stated by the Torah. When these calculations are later found to be false, people end up losing their faith Hashem because they believed in one person's misrepresentation of the Torah.

This tendency was especially prevalent, for example, during the Coronavirus outbreak in the year 2020. Many people tried discovering hints alluding to the outbreak and promising people that Mashiaḥ was imminently coming. From its very onset, Rav Ben-Haim made it very clear that making such claims was a grave mistake.[42] In the moment, predicting Mashiaḥ would put people on a short-lived high, with the expectation that everything would come true as those individuals promised. Yet in the end, all that was left

---

[41] Bereshit 47:28 quoting Bereshit Rabbah 96:1
[42] See his Youtube video from that time:
https://www.youtube.com/watch?v=8AZF1fb8dOI

was disappointment and frustration at how the "guarantees" of Mashiaḥ coming were not fulfilled. This was an injustice to those good sincere Jews who believed them, only to have their hopes crushed.

The Rambam[43] famously lists the thirteen principles of faith that every Jew must believe. One of those principles is that we must expect and yearn for Mashiaḥ to come at any moment. Mashiaḥ can arrive any day, any time, and we yearn and pray for Mashiaḥ to come as soon as possible. However, we must not focus too much on trying to calculate and uncover deeper understandings to determine when Mashiaḥ will come. These matters are hidden from us, and they will happen at the appropriate time that Hashem deems. In the meantime, we must observe all of Hashem's mitzvot with complete faith that Mashiaḥ will come at the right time. May Mashiaḥ come soon and speedily in our days, Amen.

---

[43] Perush Hamishnayot Introduction to Perek Ḥelek, Principle #12

Penine Ḥaim

SHEMOT

Penine Ḥaim

פרשת שמות

Parashat Shemot

Securing Our Future as a Nation

וְעַתָּה לְכָה וְאֶשְׁלָחֲךָ אֶל פַּרְעֹה וְהוֹצֵא אֶת עַמִּי בְנֵי יִשְׂרָאֵל מִמִּצְרָיִם :

"Come, now, and I will send you to Pharaoh, and you shall free My people, the Jews, from Egypt."[44]

The Jewish people were enslaved in Egypt for many years. They were so entrenched in slavery that it was difficult to even imagine being redeemed. How did they merit to be redeemed from their servitude? The Midrash[45] notes that there were four essential elements that set them apart from everyone else in Egypt : 1) The Jewish people continued to name their children with Jewish names, 2) they kept loyal to the Hebrew language and they did not change their spoken language, 3) they did not speak slander against each other, and 4) they kept purity in their relationships and did not intermarry with the gentiles. All of these elements instilled a strong

---

[44] Shemot 3:10
[45] Vayikra Rabba 32:5

sense of Jewish identity and preserved proper boundaries with the gentiles to prevent assimilation.

These four elements identified by the Midrash, making sure our children have Jewish names, keeping the holy language of Hebrew alive, refraining from Lashon Hara against each other, and refraining from intermarriage, are the four key ingredients to maintaining our Jewish identity when we are outside of Israel. If the Jewish people had not held on to these four critical elements when they were in Egypt, their children would have completely assimilated and become Egyptian *has veshalom*. When the time would come for Moshe Rabbenu to be sent to save them, there would be no Jewish nation to save, since they would not have even maintained a Jewish identity.

As Jews who are living in the Diaspora, we must keep these four critical elements in mind if we want to survive for the future. When the Iranian Jews, especially the Mashadi Jews, were in Iran, the most important value to them was to be steadfast not to intermarry. This is one of the main reasons that our community continues to thrive to this very day. The only way to save our generation and fight against intermarriage is through proper Jewish education. We must educate our children with proper Torah knowledge from a young age. We must all keep our Jewish names, we must all strive to know how to read and speak Hebrew, we must all be united and not speak Lashon Hara about each other, and we must make sure to only marry Jewish. Rambam[46] stresses that we must understand the severity of intermarriages. If one *has veshalom* has extra-marital relations with a Jewish woman, the child will under most conditions be considered an illegitimate child (*mamzer*), yet at the very least the child is considered his child. An illegitimate child cannot marry into the

---

[46] Halachot Issure Biah 12:7

Jewish community, but at least is still considered to be Jewish for all purposes. If a Jewish man intermarries with a gentile woman, however, the children are not even considered to be his children. They do not even inherit him; they are lost and are no longer part of the Jewish nation.

The Jews in Egypt may have fallen to a spiritually low level, but they did not let go of the core elements of their Jewish identity. They stood strong to their basic principles and did not intermarry. In this merit, they were ultimately redeemed from Egypt. May we always merit to keep our Jewish identity strong, so that we see blessing and good fortune in our future.

פרשת וארא

Parashat Va'era

Open Miracles and Hidden Miracles

וָאֵרָא אֶל אַבְרָהָם אֶל יִצְחָק וְאֶל יַעֲקֹב בְּאֵ-ל שַׁ-דָּי וּשְׁמִי ה' לֹא נוֹדַעְתִּי לָהֶם:

"I appeared to Avraham, to Yitzḥak and to Yaakov as E-l Sha-ddai, but with My Name Hashem I did not make Myself known to them"[47]

This week's Parasha records the first seven of the ten plagues that led to the Exodus of the Jewish people from Egypt. Before the beginning of the ten plagues, Hashem informs Moshe Rabbenu of how He revealed Himself in different ways in this world. Up until this point, Hashem had only appeared to our forefathers as the name "E-l Sha-ddai," but now, Hashem would reveal Himself in his four-letter name, known as the Tetragrammaton). This four-letter name was a Divine name which was never shown to our forefathers, Avraham, Yitzḥak, or Yaakov. In what way was Hashem now going to appear differently to Moshe Rabbenu than He did to our

---

[47] Shemot 6:3

forefathers? What is the significance of these names of Hashem, and what does this passage mean?

Ramban[48] explains these verses beautifully. Ramban explains that the name "E-l Sha-ddai," signifies Hashem's intervention in this world within the confines of the laws of nature. Hashem appeared to our forefathers through the lens of "E-l Sha-ddai." In other words, Hashem orchestrated tremendous miracles for our forefathers to support them throughout their lives; however, these miracles and interventions were never performed in a way that subverted the laws of nature as we know them. For example, Hashem saved our forefathers from starvation, he helped them succeed in war and in dealing with their enemies, and he helped them attain wealth and honor. While these were all interventions that were part of the Divine providence our forefathers were received, none of them were done in a way that subverted the laws of nature as we know them; rather, they were performed in a "hidden" way that Hashem's intervention would not be easily recognizable as coming from Hashem. According to the Ramban, Hashem's revelation of Himself as "E-l Sha-ddai" can be compared to the blessings and curses which are stated later in the Torah. When we follow the Torah and are rewarded for our mitzvot, or we do not follow the Torah and face consequences for our sins, Hashem delivers our reward or punishment through miracles and various interventions. However, most of the time, these miracles are hidden; to the average person, it might appear that nature is just taking its course. Hashem is performing hidden miracles by intervening in a way that we will not recognize so easily.

In contrast, Hashem tells Moshe Rabbenu that He would now reveal Himself in Egypt in a complete and most clear way - as His four-

---

[48] Ramban Shemot 6:2

letter name, the Tetragrammaton. This name of Hashem represents complete Divine revelation in the supernatural manner, where Hashem shows that He can override all the natural laws of the universe in favor of those whom He chooses. The miracles are no longer hidden; they are supernatural and clearly the work of Hashem's intervention to all those who see them. This revelation of Hashem appears throughout the ten plagues, through the miracle of the splitting of Yam Suf, and through Hashem's revelation on Har Sinai. The Midrash[49] teaches that what a simple maidservant saw at the splitting of the sea, even the great prophets Yishayahu and Yeḥezkel, as well as all other prophets, did not see in their prophecies. These miracles showed Hashem's direct providence and complete control over the universe in a way that even our forefathers had never seen. Even the most powerful empire of the time was brought to its knees at the hands of a few defenseless slaves who had the support of Hashem on their side.

We must learn and understand that Hashem's providence in this world exists in all types of ways. Most often, Hashem intervenes in this world in the hidden manner, where it is not abundantly clear to all that Hashem is performing miracles for us. At the same time, even nowadays, Hashem sometimes performs open and clear miracles that cannot be understood through natural means. With abundant prayers and observance of Hashem's mitzvot, Hashem performs both hidden and open miracles in our favor. We must strengthen ourselves in our Emunah and observance of mitzvot and always remember that Hashem oversees the world with His infinite knowledge and power that we cannot fully comprehend.

---

[49] Mechilta Masechta DeShira Beshalaḥ Parasha 2

פרשת בא

Parashat Bo

The Deeper Meaning of True Freedom

הַחֹדֶשׁ הַזֶּה לָכֶם רֹאשׁ חֳדָשִׁים רִאשׁוֹן הוּא לָכֶם לְחָדְשֵׁי הַשָּׁנָה:

"This month shall mark for you the beginning of the months; it shall be the first of the months of the year for you."[50]

This week's Parasha introduces the commandment to count and proclaim the new moon every month. The commandment is to number the months starting from the first month, which was the month of the Exodus (known today as Nisan). According to the Torah, the months of the year do not have names – they are only known as "the first month, the second month, the third month, etc." Only when the Jews first went into exile [when the first Bet Hamikdash was destroyed] did they also adopt the different names for the months - for example, Tammuz, Av, Elul, etc.[51] Proclaiming the new month is the very first commandment that the Jewish people received in the Torah as a nation. It was also one the few mitzvot in

---

[50] Shemot 12:2
[51] Yerushalmi Rosh Hashana 1:2, Ramban Shemot 12:1-2

the Torah that the Greeks tried abolishing for the Jews during the time of Ḥanukkah.[52] On a surface level, declaring the new months at their times does not seem like it should have this kind of distinction. What makes this mitzvah so special important and what is the significance of this mitzvah?

Ramban[53] explains that when counting the months, we always count from the month of Nissan in order that we never forget the miracles of the Exodus. For example, the months of Tishre is not called Tishre by the Torah, rather it is called "the seventh month." It is called the seventh month since it is the seventh month counted when counting from the first month, which is the month of the great miracles Hashem did for us in the Exodus. All the months of the year go back to the Exodus in this manner. The Exodus from Egypt was such a crucial part of becoming a nation that we must always keep it on our consciousness. Therefore, we place the Exodus at the head of our calendar and use it as a reference point when counting the rest of our months. This mitzvah was given as the first mitzvah to the Jews, to highlight that we must never forget the miracles that Hashem did for us. Our forefathers lived through abuse and suffering as slaves. We were redeemed, not by our own efforts or merits, but by the overwhelming love Hashem showed us by performing miracle after miracle to redeem us.

We must remember that Hashem took us out of Egypt to be a "free nation." What does it mean to be free? Being free does not mean to be undisciplined and wild by becoming slaves to our impulses. Rather, Hashem made us free to enable us to serve Him easily and wholeheartedly. The mitzvah of tefillin comes to reinforce this point. When we put tefillin on our heads and arms, we symbolize

---

[52] Megillat Antiochus
[53] Ramban Shemot 12:2

that we fully subjugate our thoughts and actions to the service of Hashem and His Torah. True freedom does not involve being a slave to our impulses and desires; rather, true freedom means to acquire the discipline and self-control to do what is good in the eyes of Hashem. As Pirke Avot[54] teaches: "There is no true free person other than one who commits himself to the Torah." This is why remembering the Exodus is such a crucial aspect of our religion. It constantly reminds us of Hashem's love for us and how He can redeem us even in the most challenging times. Additionally, remembering the Exodus reinforces our basic values: that true freedom means to subjugate all our thoughts and actions to the eternal service of Hashem.

---

[54] Pirke Avot 6:2

פרשת בשלח

Parashat Beshalaḥ

The Blessing of the Jews

וַיְהִי בְּשַׁלַּח פַּרְעֹה אֶת הָעָם וְלֹא נָחָם אֱ-לֹהִים דֶּרֶךְ אֶרֶץ פְּלִשְׁתִּים כִּי קָרוֹב הוּא
כִּי אָמַר אֱ-לֹהִים פֶּן יִנָּחֵם הָעָם בִּרְאֹתָם מִלְחָמָה וְשָׁבוּ מִצְרָיְמָה:

*"And it was when Pharaoh let the people go, God did not lead them
by way of the land of the Philistines, although it was nearer; for God
said, "The people may have a change of heart when they see war
and return to Egypt."[55]*

This week's Parasha is one of the most eventful Parashiyot in the
Torah. Pharaoh finally releases the Jews from Egypt, and we see the
final downfall of the Egyptians. Hashem splits the Yam Suf for the
Jewish nation to pass through, and the waters come crashing down
on the Egyptians who chased after them. When describing the
events, the Parasha opens with the word "*Vayhi*." The Gemara[56]
teaches that the words *Vayhi* normally indicates a sad and
unfortunate event which will follow it. The question can be asked,

---

[55] Shemot 13:17
[56] Megilah 10b

if it is true that *Vayhi* introduces unfortunate events, why does the Torah use the word *Vayhi* here? If anything, this Parasha should be one of the most joyous portions in the Torah, since this is the Parasha when the Jews are finally freed from all the pain and suffering they endured in Egypt!

The Midrash[57] notes the unusual use of the word *Vayhi* and explains that it was not the Jews who were expressing sadness or frustration for leaving Egypt; rather, Pharaoh was expressing sadness for sending the Jews out. Although the Jews were slaves in Egypt, there were many great minds and skilled professionals amongst them. Once Pharaoh freed them from Egypt, he began to realize that the main reason Egypt was thriving as a nation was because of the talents of the Jews who were in his country. When the Jews came to Egypt, they brought extraordinary blessing and Divine assistance to the country and Egypt was successful as the main world power of its time. The Torah uses the word *Vayhi* to show Pharoah's sadness in realizing tremendous loss of talented Jewish minds and skilled professionals that Egypt was going to lose as he freed the Jews.

The Maggid Midovna[58] explains that the message of this Midrash is still evident till this very day. Throughout history, every time a country welcomed and accepted the Jews, the Jews brought tremendous prosperity and advancement to the countries that hosted them. A country that hosts the Jewish people receives incredible blessing because of the Jews who live there.

It is noteworthy that Jews have contributed to society in an outsized way in comparison to our numbers. To highlight this point: of the 965 individual recipients of the Nobel Prize and the Nobel Memorial Prize in Economic Sciences between 1901 and 2023, at least 214

---

[57] Shemot Rabbah Parasha 20
[58] Mishle Yaakov, Parashat Beshalaḥ Mashal #95

have been Jewish or individuals with at least one Jewish parent, thus representing 22% of all recipients. Jews comprise only 0.2% of the world's population, which means that the Jewish share of Nobel prize recipients is 110 times their proportion of the world's population![59] Whenever the Jews were accepted into a country, the country thrived with our economic and intellectual contributions.

The same was true with Pharoah thousands of years earlier. As soon as he freed the Jewish nation, he regretted their absence from his country. We must appreciate this point to realize how unique and blessed we are as a Jewish nation. Being the chosen nation comes with a deep responsibility, and consequently, we must hold ourselves to a high standard. We must proudly bring the Torah's wisdom and ethics wherever we find ourselves, whether it be in the workplace, in school and especially in our homes. We must continue to be a light unto the nations and contribute our best to society wherever we are.

---

[59] Statistics retrieved from https://en.wikipedia.org/wiki/List_of_Jewish_Nobel_laureates, retrieved March 2024

פרשת יתרו

Parashat Yitro

From Witnessing to Believing

אָנֹכִי ה' אֱ-לֹהֶיךָ אֲשֶׁר הוֹצֵאתִיךָ מֵאֶרֶץ מִצְרַיִם מִבֵּית עֲבָדִים לֹא יִהְיֶה לְךָ
אֱ-לֹהִים אֲחֵרִים עַל פָּנַי:

*"I am Hashem your God who brought you out of the land of Egypt,
the house of bondage."[60]*

Parashat Yitro is the monumental parasha that recounts the events
of Hashem giving the Ten Commandments to the Jewish nation at
Har Sinai. The Ten Commandments are the cornerstone of the
Jewish faith and encapsulate many of the Torah's fundamental
values in just a few words.

The first commandment begins with Hashem stating that He is our
God who took us out of the land of Egypt. Ibn Ezra[61] describes that
he was approached by the famous Jewish philosopher and poet,
Rabbi Yehuda Halevi. Rabbi Yehuda Halevi asked Ibn Ezra as

---

[60] Shemot 20:2
[61] Ibn Ezra Shemot 20:2

follows: When Hashem describes himself as God at the beginning of the Ten Commandments, why does He describe Himself to the Jewish people as the "One Who brought you out of the land of Egypt?" Hashem could have easily described Himself using a much greater description, such as: "I am Hashem your God, the Creator of the universe and all the cosmos"? At first glance, creating the universe would be a more impressive description and would have been more apropos for Hashem to use when introducing the Ten Commandments. Why did Hashem identify himself with a seemingly less significant title as the One who took the Jews out of Egypt?

Ibn Ezra replied to Rabbi Yehuda Halevi that there are different levels of knowledge that individuals can attain. Of course, as Jews we believe that Hashem created the universe as the Torah says. However, the creation of the universe by Hashem did not have any human witnesses and is not provable to the average person. Therefore, Hashem described Himself as the God who took the Jewish nation out of Egypt. Every single one of the 600,000 adult men, plus women, elderly and children who stood at the foot of Har Sinai had witnessed the exodus from Egypt and all the miracles with their own eyes. Hashem chose to describe Himself in this way so that the acceptance of the Torah would be based on verified knowledge of events that are clear to everyone, not based on philosophical assertions that are not clearly apparent to all. The same Jews who witnessed the wonderous miracles in Egypt all heard Hashem speaking to them directly at Har Sinai. Judaism is the only religion that asserts God's revelation on a mass level to an entire nation. Therefore, Hashem chose to use this event in describing himself at Har Sinai, since this was a mass revelation that was undeniable. They had all seen Hashem's wonders with their own eyes. This experience formed the identity of the Jewish nation based on the most intimate way that the Jewish nation knew Hashem.

We mention the Exodus from Egypt every morning and every night in Shema, in Kiddush every Friday night, as well as in many other prayers in our liturgy. This is because our Torah is predicated on verified events in history that were witnessed firsthand by our ancestors and passed down directly to us from generation to generation. The laws of the Torah and our observance of those laws is not founded on philosophical assertions that are difficult to prove; the Torah is based on historical events that were witnessed by millions of people and passed down to their descendants. This direct experience is the highest and most intimate form of knowledge one can attain of Hashem's existence and is therefore the basis of how we accepted the Torah on Har Sinai.

פרשת משפטים

Parashat Mishpatim

Honesty in all Areas of Our Lives

מִדְּבַר שֶׁקֶר תִּרְחָק וְנָקִי וְצַדִּיק אַל תַּהֲרֹג כִּי לֹא אַצְדִּיק רָשָׁע:

"Keep far from a falsehood; do not bring death on those who are innocent and righteous, for I will not acquit the wrongdoer."[62]

In our Parasha, the Torah teaches us that importance of honesty. We must distance ourselves from falsehood in any context. The Torah states: "*Middevar sheker tirḥak*" – distance yourself from falsehood. The Kotzker Rebbe famously notes that most of the Torah's prohibitions only prohibit us from transgressing a certain action. The Torah will say, "Do not steal," or "Do not covet." Regarding falsehood, however, the Torah uses a unique expression - "distance yourself!" It is not enough simply not to lie - we must distance ourselves far from any form of falsehood and strive to maintain exceptional integrity.

---

[62] Shemot 23:7

An important setting for the application of this rule is in our own homes. The Gemara[63] teaches: "Rabbi Zera said: 'A person should not say to a child: I will give you something, and then not give it to him, because he thereby comes to teach the child to be dishonest.'" Parents must be honest and truthful with their children. For example, if a parent makes a promise to a child and does not stand by his or her word, the child will only learn that it is acceptable to lie. This would be the worst example for a parent to set. Therefore, parents should be careful to only make promises to their children that they can fulfill and then stand by their word. This way, the children will see that their parents' promises have value. As parents, we must be careful to reinforce the values of honesty and truthfulness for our children by modeling these values ourselves.

If one is always cautious regarding keeping this commandment, it brings him many blessings in other areas of life. By maintaining a standard of integrity, even though it is difficult at times, a person builds a reputation of trust amongst all those around him. Such a person will have clarity that will allow him to sleep at night, strengthened by the knowledge that he has not misled any person that day. People will also be more ready to conduct business with one who does business with utmost integrity. Above all, a Jew who maintains integrity in all areas of his life sanctifies the name of Hashem in this world, and there is no greater mitzvah than sanctifying the name of Hashem in this world.

The Talmud Yerushalmi[64] tells the story of the great Rabbi Shimon Ben Shetaḥ. The rabbi's students once purchased a donkey for him from an Arab merchant to help him with his travels. After bringing the donkey back to their rabbi, the students noticed that there was a

---

[63] Sukkah 46b
[64] Yerushalmi Bava Metziah 2:5

precious diamond tied to its neck. "Rabbi!" the students exclaimed. "We have found a diamond on the donkey's neck; you no longer need to work another day of your life! You can sell the diamond for an enormous amount and devote your life entirely to Torah study and Tzedakah." When the rabbi heard about what happened, he asked his students if the Arab merchant was aware of the diamond tied around the donkey's neck. The students replied that he was not. "If that is so," Rabbi Shimon said, "we must return the diamond to the merchant." Rabbi Shimon Ben Shetaḥ kept his word and returned the diamond to the merchant. The merchant could not believe that a person could be so honest to voluntarily return such a diamond even though no one would be able to find out. Upon receiving the diamond in return, the Arab merchant exclaimed, "Blessed be the God of Rabbi Shimon Ben Shetaḥ!" To Rabbi Shimon Ben Shetaḥ, this sanctification of Hashem's name was infinitely more precious than the value of the diamond.

פרשת תרומה

Parashat Teruma

Taking By Giving

דַּבֵּר אֶל בְּנֵי יִשְׂרָאֵל וְיִקְחוּ לִי תְּרוּמָה מֵאֵת כָּל אִישׁ אֲשֶׁר יִדְּבֶנּוּ לִבּוֹ תִּקְחוּ אֶת תְּרוּמָתִי :

"Tell the Jewish people to take for Me a donation; you shall accept gifts for Me from every person whose heart is so moved to give."[65]

The Parasha introduces the building of the Mishkan and the fundraising process for building it. Hashem commands the Jews to donate to the Mishkan using the expression *"Veyikḥu Li Teruma,"* meaning, "they shall **take** for Me a donation. Why does the Torah use such an expression of "taking" when it comes to donating? The Torah should have said they shall give a donation! The language of "taking" appears out of place.

Rashi[66] explains that in this context, "take" means that the donor should take money and separate from his general assets by

---

[65] Shemot 25:2
[66] Rashi Shemot 25:2

designating it for this holier cause of building the Mishkan. However, there is also a deeper idea being conveyed here in this phrase. The Midrash[67] teaches us a remarkable lesson: "More than the wealthy person gives to the poor, the poor really gives to the wealthy." In other words, while a wealthy donor provides physical sustenance to the poor by volunteering his time or by giving Tzedakah, the poor person actually gives the wealthy person an even greater gift - the opportunity to become generous and giving. The transformation from being self-absorbed to becoming compassionate is far more valuable than a donation itself. Giving Tzedakah trains us to reach outside ourselves, to be empathetic and take meaningful action to help others who may be in need. A donation that the pauper receives may be valued at a given number, but the gift of acquiring the qualities of compassion and generosity has no price tag.

This explains the expression of "taking" in our Parasha. One who "gives" a donation is really taking for himself, since the act of generosity is a conduit for the blessing in an individual's life. This idea can also be seen in the text of the Torah itself. In Parashat Ki Tisa, the Jews were instructed to give *Maḥatzit Hashekel* - a half shekel donation to the Mishkan. If we look at the word "*Maḥatzit*" ("half"), in Hebrew it is spelled מ ח צ י ת. The letter צ in the middle of the word stands for Tzedakah. The two letters closest to the letter צ on either side are חי, which stands for life. The two letters which are farthest from the צ are מת, which means death. This shows us that a person who gives Tzedakah brings himself closer to life, and distances himself from death. Therefore, when a person gives Tzedakah, he is really "taking" and not giving. In fact, the poor person who receives the donation may be doing him a favor by

---

[67] Vayikra Rabbah 34:8 and Rut Rabbah 5:9

receiving it! That is why the Torah says "take" for me a donation - because one who gives Tzedakah is truly taking more than he is giving.

The Gemara[68] teaches: "One who says I am contributing this coin to charity so that my son will live...is a full-fledged righteous person." This means that even when we perform an act of kindness to gain a material benefit from it, it is still considered a righteous act and we are blessed for it. We are also taught that we must perform acts of charity and kindness with a pleasant demeanor and with a smile.[69] This will allow for the receiver to not feel disparaged by receiving the charity. When we give Tzedakah in the proper way, we ultimately become "takers" due to the great blessing that comes from charity and kindness.

---

[68] Pesaḥim 8b
[69] Shulḥan Aruch Yoreh Deah 249:3

פרשת תצוה

Parashat Tetzaveh

The Blessing of Shabbat

וְאַתָּה תְּצַוֶּה אֶת בְּנֵי יִשְׂרָאֵל וְיִקְחוּ אֵלֶיךָ שֶׁמֶן זַיִת זָךְ כָּתִית לַמָּאוֹר לְהַעֲלֹת נֵר
תָּמִיד:

"You shall further instruct the Jews to bring you clear oil of beaten olives for lighting, for kindling lamps regularly."[70]

Our parasha begins with the instruction for the Kohen Gadol, the High Priest, to light the menorah. Even today, the menorah is still one of the most prominent symbols in Judaism and is featured on the Emblem of Israel. Rambam[71] describes the shape of the menorah. The menorah had one prominent candle at the center known as *Ner Hamaaravi*. There were six other candles, three on each side. The lights of these six candles faced inwards, towards the center candle. The *Ner Hamaaravi* was lit first, and its flame was used to light the other six candles.[72]

---

[70] Shemot 27:20
[71] Halachot Bet Habeḥira 3:8
[72] Rambam Perush Hamishnayot Tamid 6:1

Ben Ish Ḥai [73] notes that this arrangement holds deep symbolic meaning. The *Ner Hamaaravi* represents the day of Shabbat, while the other six candles symbolize the other six days of the week. Some people mistakenly believe that Shabbat is simply a day of rest, disconnected from the rest of the week. The truth is that the observance Shabbat serves as the source of blessing for all other days of the week.

Rav Ben-Haim illustrated this point with an example from American Jewish history. In the early 20th century in the United States, Saturday was conventionally considered part of the regular workweek. Employers expected all their employees to work on Shabbat. Many Jewish immigrants were faced with a difficult choice: work on Shabbat and maintain their jobs or observe Shabbat and risk losing their income. Those who compromised their Shabbat observance and worked on Shabbat, often remained low-wage employees on a fixed salary and only experienced limited financial growth. On the other hand, those who chose to observe Shabbat were often forced to start their own businesses so that they could avoid working on Shabbat. As self-employed entrepreneurs, they often achieved greater financial success than they could have ever achieved as low-wage employees. Observance of Shabbat was their greatest blessing.

Rav Ben-Haim related a personal story from his childhood growing up in the Bet Yisrael neighborhood in Yerushalayim. In their neighborhood, everyone observed Shabbat. One day, a young man in the neighborhood began working as taxi driver. The entire neighborhood was distraught to learn that this young man was unfortunately working and driving on Shabbat. One of the rabbis in the neighborhood, Rabbi Sasson Levy z"l, approached the young

---

[73] Ben Ish Ḥai Halachot Year 2 Parashat Pekude

man and asked him about his decision to work on Shabbat. After all, his parents and grandparents were all righteous individuals who always kept Shabbat. Why should he start working and not observe Shabbat? The man explained that he had many financial pressures to support his family and he needed to work all seven days of the week to pay his bills. The rabbi proposed a deal: the man would abstain from working on Shabbat and would track all of his expenses from that day until Rosh Hashana. Before Rosh Hashana, the rabbi would all his losses. And so it was. When Rosh Hashana came, the man did not approach the rabbi for any payment. The rabbi approached him to ask about the losses. The man replied, "Rabbi, the truth of the matter is that these past few months I did make less money than I usually make because I did not work all seven days of the week. However, I also noticed that there was a surprising increase in blessings in my life since I started keeping Shabbat. My normal expenses in different areas such home maintenance and family expenses were significantly less than usual. The reduced expenses actually led to a net gain, despite the decrease in my lower gross income." The rabbi jokingly remarked, "Now you owe me the net gain!"

The central lesson is that all blessings in our lives stem from the observance of Shabbat. We should never think for even a moment that observance of Shabbat could be a source of loss for us. The same way that the *Ner Hamaaravi* supplied the light for the other candles, Shabbat observance supplies the blessing for the rest of the week.

פרשת כי תשא

Parashat Ki Tisa

Transformation Through Commitment

וַיִּקַּח מִיָּדָם וַיָּצַר אֹתוֹ בַּחֶרֶט וַיַּעֲשֵׂהוּ עֵגֶל מַסֵּכָה וַיֹּאמְרוּ אֵלֶּה אֱ-לֹהֶיךָ יִשְׂרָאֵל
אֲשֶׁר הֶעֱלוּךָ מֵאֶרֶץ מִצְרָיִם :

*"This he took from them and cast in a mold and made it into a molten
calf. And they exclaimed, 'This is your god O Israel, who brought
you out of the land of Egypt.'"*[74]

This week's Parasha features the infamous sin of the Golden Calf.
Many of the commentators on the Torah are perplexed by the
obvious question: how is it possible that the Jews in the desert came
to worship the Golden Calf? They saw Hashem's open miracles
daily. The Jews all saw Hashem subvert the laws of nature for them
with Ten Plagues in Egypt. They saw Hashem split the Yam Suf for
them and drown the Egyptians with their own eyes. They
experienced direct prophecy at Har Sinai. They received Manna,
food that fell from Heaven daily. How could it be that they came to

---

[74] Shemot 32:4

such a low point to betray Hashem and commit the sin of idol worship? Rashi[75] explains that the ones who initially instigated the idol worship were the Erev Rav (a large group of Egyptians who followed the Jews in the desert), not the Jewish people themselves. Only once the Erev Rav instigated the worship were they able to convince the rest of the Jews to join them and worship as well.

The question of how the Jews came to worship a Golden Calf remains a strong question. However, there is a profound lesson we can learn from this story: miracles do not change people. Miracles can be likened to pouring gas on the floor and lighting it on fire. It may create a tremendous flame, but after a short time, the flame is gone and there is no remnant of the fire. Miracles only inspire a person for a short period of time. Long-lasting change can only come from proper education and consistent devotion.

In the times of the early Baale Hatosafot (early 12th century France), the Jewish people did not see any open miracles. The European Jewish communities saw the opposite: they suffered many persecutions, particularly at the hands of the Crusaders. Nonetheless, rather than converting to any other religion or worshipping idols, they gave their lives to remain loyal to Judaism. The Daat Zekenim[76] notes that some individuals would even slaughter their own children during the times of the Crusades, so that their children would not convert to another religion (Note: the practice of slaughtering children in such a manner was condemned by many great rabbis and it is halachically unacceptable to engage in such practices. The Daat Zekenim commentary itself notes that many rabbis prohibited the practice and tells the story of a rabbi who slaughtered young children for this purpose and was then severely

---

[75] Rashi Shemot 32:4
[76] Daat Zekenim MiBaale Hatosafot Bereshit 9:5

punished by Heaven for it. Nonetheless, the fact that some individuals were willing to go so far shows the incredible commitment that they had to ensure that their children should not leave Judaism at any cost). The secret to their dedication was due to their strong education and love of Torah. Rav Ben-Haim shared that he read in the works of the famous traveler Rabbi Binyamin of Tudela, who visited the towns in France where the Baale Hatosafot lived in that time. Even though they lived in small towns, Rabbi Binyamin of Tudela was amazed by their passion and commitment to learn Torah every day and night. Even without seeing any miracles, even when they suffered from persecutions, they remained steadfastly committed to Torah and to the worship of Hashem.

The generation of Jews in the desert who were saved by miracles and saw the hand of Hashem every day did not have the same commitment that the Baale Hatosafot had. The miracles did not work to change them, because miracles do not change people. They cannot replace the hard work that is put in every day to consistently devote oneself to Hashem. Only the daily commitment to Torah and Judaism can ultimately truly transform a person in the long term.

Rav Ben-Haim vividly describes the miracles he saw with his own eyes during the Six Day War in 1967. Everyone saw the miracles and the open Hand of Hashem. Many secular Jews openly admitted that the victory did not make any logical sense from a military perspective and only happened due to Divine intervention. For a short time, even some of the most secular people were inspired. In the end of the day, although some people became religious after the Six Day War, most people did not change. After a few days, those who did not keep Shabbat went back to desecrating the Shabbat. Those who did not keep kosher went back to not keeping kosher.

This is because they were not consistently working on educating themselves and building long term change.

We must emphasize the importance of educating our children in Torah and building long term growth for the next generation. It is not enough to show external respect for the Torah; we must also encourage our children to study and follow the Torah. The Rambam[77] notes that Hashem is different from human beings. While human beings themselves are separate from their intelligence (human beings and their intelligence are two separate entities), Hashem and His intelligence are all one and the same entity. Therefore, when a person learns Torah regularly, he or she connects with Hashem directly in the most direct way possible.

Waiting for a miracle will rarely accomplish anything; even when a miracle happens, a person usually will not change. On the other hand, consistent devotion to Torah study will greatly improve a person in the long-term. The next generation can only be built with the strongest Jewish education, with an emphasis on consistent dedication for an appreciation for Torah values and ideals.

---

[77] Halachot Teshuva 5:11

פרשת ויקהל

Parashat Vayakhel

Donating With the Purest Intentions

קְחוּ מֵאִתְּכֶם תְּרוּמָה לַה׳ כֹּל נְדִיב לִבּוֹ יְבִיאֶהָ אֵת תְּרוּמַת ה׳ זָהָב וָכֶסֶף וּנְחֹשֶׁת:

"Take from among you gifts to Hashem, anyone whose heart is moved, shall bring the Hashem's donation, silver, gold, copper."[78]

Rav Ben-Haim related the following story: When Rav Yitzḥak of Volozhin headed the famed Volozhin Yeshiva, he once sent an individual to collect money for the Yeshiva from a philanthropist who had helped the Yeshiva in the past. The messenger was dressed respectably in very nice clothes and sent off in a beautiful chariot. When the messenger arrived at the philanthropist's home, the philanthropist told him, "I am sorry, I cannot help the Yeshiva at this time." When the messenger returned to Rav Yitzḥak, the rabbi could not believe that he was turned down. The philanthropist was a committed donor to the Yeshiva for many years. Rav Yitzḥak decided he must visit the donor himself.

---

[78] Shemot 35:5

When Rav Yitzḥak arrived, the donor explained the reason he did not donate. "In the past, when the Yeshiva was poor, I gave joyfully because I knew that whatever I donated went directly to the needs of the students of the Yeshiva. The messenger of the Yeshiva would come in the humblest clothes and travel accommodations. However, now that you send a messenger in grandeur, I do not want to donate! I would like my donations to go for students learning in Yeshiva, not for the luxury accommodations of fundraisers!" The philanthropist was concerned about how his donations would be allocated now that the Yeshiva seemed to be doing well and could afford luxury accommodations for its staff.

Rav Yitzḥak told the philanthropist the following: in our Parasha, the chief architect of the Mishkan was none other than Betzalel. Betzalel was no ordinary artisan. His talent was Divinely inspired, and he intuitively understood deep calculations. The Gemara[79] teaches that Betzalel's name is derived from בצל א-ל, i.e. "in the shadow of Hashem." This means that Betzalel was endowed with Divine wisdom to know exactly how Hashem wanted the Mishkan to be built.

What exactly was this Divine wisdom? Rav Yitzḥak of Volozhin explained that Betzalel understood exactly where to place each donation for the Mishkan based on the intention and motivation of each donor. For example, if a widow came and donated a small amount of gold, but she gave it with all her heart, Betzalel was able to see that, and he would set aside the gold she donated towards the holiest utensil of the Mishkan, the Aron (Holy Ark of the Tabernacle). On the other hand, if a wealthy person donated money only because of social pressure, in order not to get embarrassed, Betzalel used that donation for less important external pieces, such

---

[79] Berachot 55a

as the gold-plating of the boards or for the clasps of the curtains. "Likewise," Rav Yitzḥak concluded, "when you donate with the pure intent to help the students of the Yeshiva, we will make sure your donation goes directly to our students! The chariots and luxury accommodations will not come from your money; those come from those who donate for sake of the grandiosity of their donations."

The lesson from this story is that when one gives with all his heart, his money will go to the most meaningful cause. We should not give charity with a sad or upset demeanor. Rather, we should give it in a pleasant manner and with the most genuine intentions. When given with the correct intentions, the money will go to the place where it will be used best and will correspond to the intention of our donations. When we give charity wholeheartedly, Hashem will place worthwhile causes before us so that our Tzedakah will ultimately go to the best place.

פרשת פקודי

Parashat Pekude

Loving Every Jew

וַיָּשֶׂם אֹתָם עַל כִּתְפֹת הָאֵפֹד אַבְנֵי זִכָּרוֹן לִבְנֵי יִשְׂרָאֵל כַּאֲשֶׁר צִוָּה ה' אֶת מֹשֶׁה:

"They were set on the shoulder pieces of the Ephod, as stones of remembrance for the Jews - as Hashem had commanded Moshe."[80]

The Kohen Gadol's outfit was one of the most special outfits to be worn by any person. Among his unique garments, there were two articles of clothing which had the names of all twelve tribes inscribed on them. First, the Kohen Gadol was required to wear the *Ḥoshen*, a breastplate which contained twelve precious stones, each with the name of one tribe inscribed on it. Second, the apron of the Kohen Gadol, known as the *Ephod*, had two shoulder straps to hold it in place. Each of the shoulder straps contains one of two Shoham stones, two gemstones that were inscribed with the names of all twelve tribes (six on each stone). Why does the Torah insist that the

---

[80] Shemot 37:9

Kohen Gadol's garments must consist of the names of the twelve
Jewish tribes?

The Torah is teaching a profound lesson. By inscribing the names of
the Jewish people on the shoulders of the Kohen Gadol, the Torah
was teaching us that Jewish leaders must carry the weight of entire
Jewish people on their shoulders without differentiating between
different types of Jews. The responsibility of the Kohen Gadol is to
serve the entire Jewish nation. His role as a leader is not for him to
indulge in his personal honor. Rather, he must love every Jew as his
own and be sensitive to the needs of all types of Jews regardless of
their background or social status. This was the depth behind the
Kohen Gadol carrying stones inscribed with all twelve tribes. The
Kohen Gadol must have unwavering sensitivity to the needs of the
entire Jewish nation as a whole.

Rav Ben-Haim noted that a beautiful story is told about the late
Lubavitcher Rebbe, Rav Menaḥem Mendel Schneerson z"l. The
Rebbe was known for his custom of distributing a dollar bill to those
who would visit him outside of his office. He would then encourage
them to give Tzedakah to the charity of their choice. Even in his old
age, he would stand up during his visiting hours while he distributed
a dollar bill to each person. His students would plead with him to sit
during these hours, especially since these visits would usually
extend to several hours at a time. The Rebbe refused to sit and
explained: "When a person counts diamonds, he does not get tired.
Every Jew who comes to me is like a diamond. Every time I have
the honor of interacting with another Jew, I am infused with energy
and do not get tired when I see them."

As Jews, we should always be inspired by the lesson of the stones
of the Kohen Gadol. We must learn to love and be prepared to assist
every Jew who is in need. The same way the Kohen Gadol was

instructed to be sensitive to the needs of all Jews regardless of their ethnic background or social status, we should be sensitive to the needs of every Jew in the same way. This lesson is especially applicable for Jewish leaders, but even applies to every one of us in our daily lives as well.

VAYIKRA

Penine Ḥaim

פרשת ויקרא

Parashat Vayikra

Between Man and Man

נֶפֶשׁ כִּי תֶחֱטָא וּמָעֲלָה מַעַל בַּה' וְכִחֵשׁ בַּעֲמִיתוֹ בְּפִקָּדוֹן אוֹ בִתְשׂוּמֶת יָד אוֹ בְגָזֵל אוֹ עָשַׁק אֶת עֲמִיתוֹ:

"When a person sins and commits a treachery against Hashem by dealing deceitfully with another in the matter of a deposit or a pledge, or through robbery, or by defrauding another."[81]

In our Parasha, the Torah introduces to the commandment of offering guilt sacrifices for theft. The Torah says that if a person falsely swore regarding a pledge or a loan or robbery and is later found to be lying, he must offer an *Asham* offering (guilt offering) to atone for his sin. When looking carefully at the text, one cannot help but see the interesting language the Torah uses to describe this sin. The Torah says that by falsely denying the loan or robbery, the individual is committing a sin which is considered *"Ma'al BaHashem,"* a treachery against Hashem. On the surface, this does

---

[81] Vayikra 5:21

not seem accurate. The one who swears falsely and lies in this scenario commits a sin towards a fellow man, not towards Hashem! What does this verse teach us?

The answer is that the Torah is teaching us that committing a sin to our fellow neighbor is, by definition, also a sin towards Hashem. That means that when a person causes pain to his fellow friend, he is not only sinning to his friend – he is sinning to Hashem as well. This idea can also be seen by the halacha that on Yom Kippur, if a person commits a sin to his fellow Jew, the sinner must do teshuva to receive forgiveness, both from the friend and from Hashem.[82] Causing damage to another Jew is a grave sin to Hashem as well and it requires a formal teshuva process similar to a sin directly against Hashem.

We can see the gravity of hurting another person's feelings through the story Ḥannah and Penina in the book of Shemuel.[83] Penina would insult Ḥannah and make her feel bad for not having any children. The Gemara[84] teaches that Penina had good intentions when she would insult Ḥannah. She wanted to encourage Ḥannah to pray to Hashem in a more heartfelt way, so that her prayers would be answered. Even though she may have had good intentions, Penina was punished for her actions. Every time Ḥannah got pregnant, Penina lost one of her children.

This story of Ḥannah and Penina teaches us that playing with a person's feelings is like playing with explosives. Any action which brings pain to another Jew is akin to any of the other sins in the Torah against Hashem and has serious repercussions. We must be careful with the way we interact with our fellow Jews. Even if

---

[82] Rambam Hilchot Teshuva 2:8-9
[83] Shemuel 1 1:1-7
[84] Bava Batra 16a

someone else happens to hurt us first, we should do our best not to respond in the same manner. The Gemara[85] beautifully teaches: those who are insulted and do not insult, who hear their shame and do not respond...regarding them, the verse says: "And they that love Him are as the sun going forth in its might." When we treat our interactions with others as being a sacred responsibility just as any other responsibility we have towards Hashem, we should merit to have peace and harmony in our lives.

---

[85] Shabbat 88b

פרשת צו

Parashat Tzav

The Purpose of Korbanot

צַו אֶת אַהֲרֹן וְאֶת בָּנָיו לֵאמֹר זֹאת תּוֹרַת הָעֹלָה הִוא הָעֹלָה עַל מוֹקְדָה עַל הַמִּזְבֵּחַ
כָּל הַלַּיְלָה עַד הַבֹּקֶר וְאֵשׁ הַמִּזְבֵּחַ תּוּקַד בּוֹ :

*"Command Aharon and his sons thus: This is the ritual of the burnt
offering: The burnt offering itself shall remain where it is burned
upon the altar all night until morning, while the fire on the altar is
kept going on it."*[86]

This week's Parasha describes various korbanot and their detailed
laws. The Haftara of this week's Parasha, which comes from the
book of Yirmiyahu, gives us a powerful message regarding the
korbanot. The Haftara contains the following rebuke towards the
Jewish nation:
*"For I did not speak with your forefathers, nor did I command them
on the day I brought them out of the land of Egypt concerning burnt*

---

[86] Vayikra 6:2

or peace offerings. Rather it was only this thing that I commanded them, saying, 'Listen to My voice, that I will be your God and you will be My people and you will go on the entire way that I command you.'" [87]

This passage seems odd at first glance. Almost the entire Sefer Vayikra, a full book of the five books of the Torah, discusses numerous commandments regarding offering korbanot. How can the prophet Yirmiyahu claim that Hashem did not command the Jews at all regarding korbanot, but only to "follow His ways?"

The answer lies in understanding the purpose of korbanot. What exactly is a korban all about? When a Jew committed a sin, he would bring a korban in the Bet Hamikdash, as commanded in the Torah. The Kohen would perform sheḥita on the animal. The individual was meant to look at the blood of the korban and think, "The punishment for the sin that I have committed is like the slaughtering of that animal. I myself should have been slaughtered in its stead." These thoughts guide the sinner towards repentance. They are meant to generate feelings of remorse and propel the individual to come closer to Hashem. The main reason for offering korbanot for sins is that as a result, the person changes himself. Korbanot are a medium through which the sinner undergoes a transformation and removes himself from sin. [88]

In the times of Yirmiyahu, korbanot were unfortunately not being practiced genuinely. People would go through the motions of bringing korbanot but were not sincere in their repentance. Instead of using them as a medium towards teshuva, they used korbanot as an excuse for their own misdeeds. Therefore, Hashem criticized the

---

[87] Yirmiyahu 7:22
[88] Ramban Vayikra 1:9, see also Rabbi Joseph B. Soloveitchik, On Repentance, pp. 266-268

nation through Yirmiyahu by saying that these empty gestures are not at all what Hashem seeks from them. Regarding such insincere gestures, the prophet Yishayahu similarly criticized, *"Who asked that of you to Trample My courtyards? No more; bringing offerings is futile, incense is offensive to Me."*[89]

The Gemara[90] teaches that Hashem seeks the heart of a Jew. The sacrifices were meant to be a means to awaken an individual's mind and heart to come closer to Hashem. So too, when we perform mitzvot, we must always be genuine and sincere when performing them. We should not allow the mitzvot to become a habitual routine without any heartfelt awareness. Instead, we should always direct our hearts and minds to allow mitzvot to be transformative experiences to bring us closer to Hashem and His Torah.

---

[89] Yishayahu 1:11-13
[90] Sanhedrin 106b

פרשת שמיני

Parashat Shemini

A Lesson in Respect

וַיִּקְחוּ בְנֵי אַהֲרֹן נָדָב וַאֲבִיהוּא אִישׁ מַחְתָּתוֹ וַיִּתְּנוּ בָהֵן אֵשׁ וַיָּשִׂימוּ עָלֶיהָ קְטֹרֶת
וַיַּקְרִבוּ לִפְנֵי ה' אֵשׁ זָרָה אֲשֶׁר לֹא צִוָּה אֹתָם:

"And Aharon's sons, Nadav and Avihu, each took his pan, put fire in them, and placed incense upon it, and they brought before Hashem a foreign fire, which He had not commanded them." [91]

This week's Parasha recounts the unfortunate incident of Nadav and Avihu, the two sons of Aharon. On the most joyous day of the Mishkan's inauguration, they acted rashly and performed a service that was not commanded to them. A fire erupted from Hashem's presence and tragically consumed them both.

How did Nadav and Avihu come to commit such actions, which caused them both to die so tragically on one of the happiest days for the entire nation? The Gemara[92] offers one explanation: "Nadav said

---

[91] Vayikra 6:2
[92] Sanhedrin 52a

to Avihu, 'When will these two elders, Moshe and Aharon, finally die already, so that you and I can lead the generation?' Hashem responded to them, 'Let us see who will bury whom.'" In the end, they as children did not bury their father. Instead, their father Aharon and Moshe ended up burying them. Rav Pappa explained this with a proverb that people would say: "There are many old camels that are loaded with the skins of young camels." In other words, we naturally expect the older generation to pass away before the younger generation. Yet, this does not always happen. Sometimes, tragedy strikes, and the younger generation dies first, and the parents must bury their children. The Gemara teaches that this can sometimes happen when the younger generation disrespects their elders. Hashem's response, "Let us see who will bury whom," is a consequence of this disrespect.

The Gemara's lesson is powerful. Unfortunately, it is a common phenomenon for younger generations to feel entitled and superior to their elders. They may view their parents or older relatives as being slow, outdated and out of touch in their methods. Feeling modern and enlightened, they also believe they have the license to disrespect the elders.

However, nothing could be farther from the truth. Even when disagreeing with the elders, it is essential to maintain the dignity and respect of the previous generation, especially one's parents or grandparents. The Torah prohibits disrespecting our elders, stating: "You shall stand up before the aged and show deference to the old; You shall fear Me, I am Hashem." [93] Respecting the older generation brings blessings with it. When the younger generation gives the proper respect and deference to the older generation, Hashem

---

[93] Vayikra 19:32

blesses them to receive respect from the next younger generation in their own old age.

פרשת תזריע

Parashat Tazria

Tzaraat and Lashon Hara

אָדָם כִּי יִהְיֶה בְעוֹר בְּשָׂרוֹ שְׂאֵת אוֹ סַפַּחַת אוֹ בַהֶרֶת וְהָיָה בְעוֹר בְּשָׂרוֹ לְנֶגַע צָרָעַת
וְהוּבָא אֶל אַהֲרֹן הַכֹּהֵן אוֹ אֶל אַחַד מִבָּנָיו הַכֹּהֲנִים:

"When a person has on the skin of the body a swelling, a rash, or a discoloration, and it develops into a scaly affection on the skin of the body, it shall be reported to Aharon the priest or to one of his sons, the priests."[94]

The laws of *Tzaraat* are some of the most fascinating laws in the Torah. Rambam[95] writes that the phenomenon of *Tzaraat* is not a typical medical condition caused by a disease or virus. Rather, it is a spiritual phenomenon which has physical manifestations that appear like leprosy on the body, or on a person's clothing, or on the walls of a person's home. *Tzaraat*, however, was not a bacterium or virus that could spread by natural means. It was a spiritual disease

---

[94] Vayikra 13:2
[95] Rambam Halachot Tumat Tzaraat 16:10

which was regulated by Hashem as a sign for the Jewish people to learn and do teshuva.

To illustrate, the Mishna[96] says that a Ḥatan (a groom) who is found to have *Tzaraat* would not be examined by the Kohen to evaluate the nature of the discoloration on the skin. Rather, they push off the evaluation of the potential *Tzaraat* till after the seven days of celebration that follow the wedding. This protects the bride and groom's celebration from any difficult news which would negatively impact the joy that the couple should feel at this important stage of their lives. If *Tzaraat* was a natural medical phenomenon, then the last thing we would allow would be for a groom to spread a contagious disease to many others present at the wedding. This is one law that illustrates that *Tzaraat* was not a physical disease, it was a spiritual disease caused by spiritual factors.

The Gemara[97] enumerates many different reasons why the punishment of *Tzaraat* would be decreed on an individual. The most notable of them was the sin of Lashon Hara, harmful speech. When a person was declared by the Kohen to have *Tzaraat*, he was left in solitude outside of the Jewish community. It was prohibited to greet the *Metzora,* and anyone who would come close to the *Metzora* during the days of his impurity would become impure as well. All of this was meant to teach a lesson to the *Metzora.* The *Metzora* damaged the reputation of individuals unnecessarily by saying Lashon Hara and caused division amongst the Jewish people. The consequence of his actions was that he would be forced into solitude where nobody would want to speak to him for a period of time, and that way he would understand the harm that he caused to others.

---

[96] Negaim 3:2
[97] Arachin 16a

Rav Ben-Haim noted that the story is told that someone once asked the saintly Ḥafetz Ḥaim (who brought great awareness to the laws of Lashon Hara by his famous Sefer Ḥafetz Ḥaim) the following question: "Rabbi, you worked so hard to write books and to educate people about the severity of Lashon Hara. But what did you accomplish? Just go to any synagogue on any given day. Unfortunately to our great dismay, many people continue to speak Lashon Hara! So, what have you really accomplished with your life's work?" The Ḥafetz Ḥaim answered, "Even if I saved one synagogue from speaking Lashon Hara, it was enough for my efforts." He left the man but then returned to the man and corrected himself: "Even if I saved one person from speaking or listening to Lashon Hara at any time, it was worth all of my efforts." We must learn to refrain from speaking Lashon Hara and to judge others favorably, whether it be our family members, our friends, or our leaders. Learning to see others in a positive light will help us achieve peace within our communities and families and help us achieve inner peace for ourselves as well.

פרשת מצורע

Parashat Metzora

The Power of Speech

זֹאת תִּהְיֶה תּוֹרַת הַמְּצֹרָע בְּיוֹם טָהֳרָתוֹ וְהוּבָא אֶל הַכֹּהֵן׃

"This shall be the law of the Metzora on the day of his purification: He shall be brought to the Kohen." [98]

There are many wonderful lessons that we can learn from the laws of *Tzaraat*. One of the most interesting laws regarding *Tzaarat* is the process of diagnosing a *Metzora* as impure. The halacha is that to be declared pure or impure, a Kohen must be the one to declare the individual impure or pure. [99] Normally, an adult Kohen is the one who makes the declaration. However, *Tzaraat* is one of the only places where even the declaration of a child or a person with a mental illness carries halachic weight. [100] For example, if there is no Kohen expert present, a rabbi [who was not a Kohen] would examine the individual. Then the rabbi would tell the Kohen to say

[98] Vayikra 14:2
[99] Rambam Hilchot Tum'at Tzaraat 9:2
[100] Arachin 3a

the word "*Tameh*," [impure] or "*Tahor*," [pure]. If there is no adult Kohen available, then a child Kohen would be brought to be present, and the rabbi would instruct the child Kohen to say "*Tahor*" or "*Tameh*." At first glance, it may seem a little childish and degrading to bring a child just to declare a diagnosis for the *Metzora*. Why is there such a unique law by *Tzaraat* and what is the lesson to be learnt from here?

In fact, there is an amazing lesson that we can learn here. The Torah here emphasizes the true power of speech and the reach our words can have. A person who speaks Lashon Hara often assumes that he did not really commit such a grave sin. Did he steal from anyone? Did he murder anyone? He did not even cause any physical harm! However, the truth is that one who speaks Lashon Hara can cause tremendous damage. In the book of Mishle,[101] Shelomo Hamelech compares one who speaks disparagingly about others as "a madman scattering deadly firebrands and arrows." This means to say that words inflict pain as much as arrows or any other physical harm. Hashem commands that such an individual must go seek a Kohen - even a young child. By this young child declaring one word of "*Tahor*" or "*Tameh*" stands the difference between purity and impurity. Purity would mean that the individual can be a normal member of the Jewish community, while being impure would mean that he would be excommunicated from the Jewish community and must live in solitude until he becomes pure. The Torah is showing the *Metzora* the power of words. With the power of speech, we can either build or destroy.

---

[101] Mishle 26:18

In the book of Mishle,[102] Shelomo Hamelech further teaches, "Death and life are in the power of the tongue." The Midrash[103] quotes a parable explaining this verse. There was once a king whose daughter was sick with a rare condition whose only cure was by drinking the milk of a lioness. A messenger of the king agreed to this task of finding and retrieving the cure for the king's daughter. Indeed, the messenger was successful in his mission of acquiring the milk of a lioness. On route to the delivery of the cure, the different limbs of the messenger started arguing over which of them was the most important to the success of the messenger's mission. The arms said that they were the most important, for they were able to grab the milk. The legs claimed they were the most important since the messenger would only be able to run to the milk and escape the lioness because of them. The tongue then argued it was the most important of all in helping the messenger succeed. All the other limbs disregarded the tongue and laughed at how unimportant it was, since the tongue doesn't even consist of any bones! When the messenger arrived at the king's palace, the tongue caused the messenger to say, "Dear king, here is the dog milk that you requested!" The king became furious at how the messenger was mocking him by bringing the milk of the dog instead of the milk of the lioness and sentenced the messenger to be executed on the spot. On the way to the death gallows, the different limbs started begging the tongue to retract what it said. They all realized the tongue's superiority over all the other limbs. The tongue then caused the man to correct himself to the king and explain that sometimes a lioness is also referred to as a dog in his native language, and that he did not intend anything disrespectful at all. The king's fury was quieted, and

---

[102] Mishle 18:21
[103] Midrash Shoher Tov Tehillim 39

he thanked the messenger for delivering the cure for his sick daughter. This is the meaning of the verse in Mishle that life and death are in the hands of the tongue. A person's fate can be determined simply by words.

The faculty of speech we have is the most elevated faculty that we have as human beings. We must appreciate the impact of our words and internalize the strength which Hashem has given us by giving us the power of speech. We should always look to use our speech to learn and teach Torah, to empower people with kind words, and to elevate the world by bringing awareness of Hashem's presence to the world at large.

פרשת אחרי מות

Parashat Aḥare Mot

Taking Responsibility for Ourselves

וַיְדַבֵּר ה' אֶל מֹשֶׁה אַחֲרֵי מוֹת שְׁנֵי בְּנֵי אַהֲרֹן בְּקָרְבָתָם לִפְנֵי ה' וַיָּמֻתוּ:

"Hashem spoke to Moshe after the death of the two sons of Aharon who died when they drew too close to the presence of Hashem:"[104]

Imagine the scene. The Jewish people are finally inaugurating the Mishkan, a home for Hashem's presence. The nation is on a high. A fire from Hashem descends to the Mishkan to consume the sacrifices that were brought, indicating Hashem's great love for the Jewish people who were all present. Suddenly, tragedy strikes. Aharon Hakohen's two sons are tragically killed by Hashem's fire. The nation is disoriented: is this day meant to be a day of mourning or happiness? The question can be asked: why did Hashem cause Aharon's sons Nadav and Avihu to publicly die on such a joyous day? The Midrash[105] lists many possibilities for why they deserved

---

[104] Vayikra 16:1
[105] Vayikra Rabba 20:8-9

to die. But the question can still be asked: why did Hashem choose such a day? If they deserved to die for their sins, was Hashem not able to wait for a different time to bring about such a tragic event in front of the entire nation?

The answer to this question may be understood by means of a profound parable from the Maggid Midovna.[106] There was once a king who built a city and decided to supply it with only the very highest quality infrastructure. He invested in building the very best buildings, roads, schools, and infrastructure that was possible at any level. One person approached the king and said, "Your majesty, there is one thing lacking in this city. You did not bring the best doctor in the world yet!" After hearing this, the king appointed a search team to find the best doctor in the world. He negotiated a salary and brought the doctor to his city, and the entire city celebrated that the greatest doctor was coming to reside with them.

On the first day that the doctor began, a patient came to him with a simple cold, and the doctor prescribed a treatment. Unfortunately, the entire city was horrified to learn that not only did the patient's condition not improve from the doctor's treatment, it worsened to the point that he had to be hospitalized! The city was in shock. The king approached the doctor in outrage: "How could you mess up!? Every mother and grandmother can treat a common cold with home remedies! How is it possible that your treatment made his condition worse?" The doctor replied to the king, "Believe it or not, I did it intentionally!" The doctor then explained himself: "When I came to the city, I saw that everyone celebrated my arrival. I also noticed that people became lax regarding taking care of their personal

---

[106] Mishle Yaakov Aḥare Mot Mashal #182. Some of the details of the story are changed in Rav Ben-Haim's account of the parable. Both accounts of the story highlight the same message.

health. Every person said: 'It is okay now for me to overeat, not to exercise, to take unhealthy risks, and to live my life any way I want. We have the greatest doctor in the world to save us from any malady!' When I noticed this, I realized that I must send a message to the people of the city. The people of the city must know that if they do not care for their personal health, I will not always be able to save them from their illnesses. Therefore, I purposely put the first patient in distress for the people of the town to learn that they must take their personal health seriously. Being healthy requires that every person watch their own personal health and not to rely on a doctor to save them."

This parable explains exactly what happened to the Jews when the Mishkan was built. Every person was excited and celebrated the building of the Mishkan and for Hashem's presence to come dwell amongst the people. At the same time, some Jews may have felt that since Hashem now dwelled among them and sacrifices were being brought on their behalf every day, this would allow them to be lax with the observance of the Mitzvot. Hashem's constant presence amongst them would entitle them to unconditional forgiveness for any sins they might do. After all, the sacrifices of the Mishkan would always be there to atone for them daily! All sins would be forgiven! Therefore, on the day the Mishkan was inaugurated, Hashem caused the sons of Aharon to die. This tragedy was meant to shock and alert the Jews. While it was a tremendous merit to have the Mishkan and have Hashem dwell among them, they still had the responsibility to observe all of Hashem's commandments in the Torah to thrive as a nation.

The take home message is clear. Even nowadays, we have the synagogue for Tefila and days such as Yom Kippur for Hashem to forgive us for our sins. While these institutions present us with tremendous blessing and opportunities, they do not absolve us of the responsibility to keep Hashem's commandments in full. There are times where even though Hashem loves us, He may not save us if we do not care spiritually for ourselves. Bearing this in mind, we should be strengthened taking responsibility to observe all of Hashem's commandments in full as the primary means of bringing blessing to our lives.

פרשת קדושים

Parashat Kedoshim

Transforming the Mundane: The Jewish Definition of Holiness

דַּבֵּר אֶל כָּל עֲדַת בְּנֵי יִשְׂרָאֵל וְאָמַרְתָּ אֲלֵהֶם קְדֹשִׁים תִּהְיוּ כִּי קָדוֹשׁ אֲנִי ה' אֱ-לֹהֵיכֶם :

"Speak to the whole Jewish community and say to them: You shall be holy, for I, Hashem your God, am holy."[107]

One of the most famous and profound phrases in the Torah appears in this week's Parasha: *"Kedoshim Tihyu"* - "You shall be Holy." However, many people struggle to understand its meaning. What exactly is this "holiness" that the Torah refers to? How does Judaism define the concept of "holiness" and how does one attain this lofty state of "holiness"?

The monumental work of the Rambam (Maimonides), the Mishneh Torah, compiled the final halachic conclusions of the Talmudic sources. He named one volume of his work the book of "Kedusha,"

---

[107] Vayikra 19:2

or holiness. If you were to ask your average person to guess which laws Rambam discussed in this book of "holiness," they might respond that it includes some laws regarding the esoteric concepts of the Bet Hamikdash, or lofty ideas about prayer or about the afterlife. However, none of these are contained in the book of Holiness. So, what makes up this "book of holiness?" Surprisingly, it contains the prohibitions of eating non-kosher food, the prohibitions of certain intimate relationships, and the laws of proper kosher slaughter. What exactly do these have to do with holiness?

Many other religions define holiness through asceticism: complete detachment oneself from worldly pleasures. According to this definition, to be holy might mean living a life secluded in a monastery, remaining celibate and not getting married for one's entire life, or engaging in frequent fasting and self-mutilation. Judaism does not accept these extreme approaches as a means towards holiness.

According to Judaism, one can, and even should engage in physical and pleasurable activity - but within the proper framework, mindset, and intentions. We are meant to eat, but not every kind of food, nor solely to satisfy cravings. Instead, we should eat to appreciate Hashem's kindness in the world and to strengthen one's body to serve Hashem.[108] Similarly, Judaism sees marriage and building a family as mitzvot that every person must strive to fulfill. Building a family brings holiness to a person's life by sanctifying his passions and by giving a person a space to learn the meaning of true love and being a role model for one's children. Hashem gave us this world to enjoy it, but we must elevate it and do so with sanctity. For example, the average person may find the carcass of a dead sheep repulsive.

---

[108] Gemara Berachot 63a, Rambam Hilchot De'ot 3:3, Shulḥan Aruch Oraḥ Ḥaim 231:1

A wise Jew, however, might take the hide and use the opportunity to write a Sefer Torah. The Sefer Torah now becomes the holiest object for the Jewish people. This exemplifies how a Jew can take even the most mundane item and elevate it to a high spiritual level. This is our purpose as Jewish people - to sanctify the material world and create a holy space for Hashem's presence in this physical world.

To illustrate further, the Midrash[109] teaches that Hashem desired a dwelling place in this world. Therefore, Hashem did not command Adam and Ḥava to completely refrain from eating all the fruits of Gan Eden. Instead, they were permitted to enjoy all the fruits except for one. In this way, they would be able to create a space for Hashem by enjoying this world and fulfilling Hashem's commandments at the same time.

By sanctifying our thoughts and physical activities, we create a space for Hashem's presence to reside in this physical world. This is Judaism's definition of holiness: elevating the physical and mundane world to a higher spiritual purpose. Therefore, the Rambam included the laws of eating and intimate relationships in the book of Kedusha since these embody the true definition of "holiness" in Judaism.

The Talmud Yerushalmi[110] tells a beautiful story of a poor student who would put aside a coin every day. His wife asked him what the purpose of this practice was. He responded that his teacher told him that we will face judgement for every permissible pleasure that we did not enjoy in this world. The husband saved money on the side so that when a new seasonal fruit came into the market, he could buy the fruit to say a beracha and praise Hashem for having the fruit. We

---

[109] Midrash Tanḥuma Naso 16
[110] Yerushalmi Kiddushin 84a

see from this story that our responsibility in this world is not to abstain from the material world, but to engage with the material world and spiritually elevate it.

פרשת אמור

Parashat Emor

Investing in the Future of Judaism

וַיֹּאמֶר ה' אֶל מֹשֶׁה אֱמֹר אֶל הַכֹּהֲנִים בְּנֵי אַהֲרֹן וְאָמַרְתָּ אֲלֵהֶם לְנֶפֶשׁ לֹא יִטַּמָּא בְּעַמָּיו :

"Hashem said to Moshe: Speak to the priests, the sons of Aharon, and say to them: None shall defile himself for any [dead] person among his kin."[111]

This week's Parasha begins with an intriguing redundancy. The verse uses the word "say" twice: "Say... and you shall say" (אמור.... ואמרת). We know well that the Torah does not repeat words for no reason. What does this double "say" signify?

Rashi[112] quotes the Gemara[113] which explains that the double expression hints at the responsibility of elders to teach all these laws to the youth (להזהיר גדולים על הקטנים). Parents are responsible for rearing their children to observe the Torah. For example, if a Kohen

---

[111] Vayikra 21:1
[112] Rashi Vayikra 21:1
[113] Yevamot 114a

needs to retrieve an object that is in the cemetery, he cannot ask his son to retrieve it for him, since his son is also a Kohen who may not enter the cemetery. Similarly, parents cannot ask their children to desecrate the Shabbat on their behalf. If the act is prohibited for the parent, the parent also may not ask a child to do it for him. In this way, parents and children share an equal responsibility in keeping the mitzvot and prohibitions of the Torah.

On a related note: regarding the vessels of the Bet Hamikdash, the halacha states that if gold is not available to make the Menorah, another basic metal can be used temporarily.[114] In fact, this is what the Maccabees did when they first won control of the Bet Hamikdash: they constructed a makeshift Menorah until they could build a new Menorah from gold. However, for the Aron Kodesh (the Ark) and for the Kapporet (the cover of the Aron), the only material that can be used is pure gold. Why this distinction?

The Aron Hakodesh is the vessel which holds up the Cherubim, symbolizing the Jewish youth. The Torah is teaching us that when it comes to the development of our youth, we may only use the finest material of all, pure gold. All other items in the Bet Hamikdash can be replaced with a different metal or material. However, we may not cut corners when it comes to the development of our children, who are represented by the Cherubim. The Torah education of our children is paramount and must only be the best of the best. That way, we can perpetuate our legacy and values from generation to generation.

Therefore, it is of highest importance for parents to send their children to the best yeshiva day school available. Even with the best yeshiva education, parents must actively teach and model Jewish

---

[114] Mechilta Debaḥodesh (Yitro) Parasha 10, Rambam Halachot Bet Habeḥira 1:18

values at home for their children. We must show our children the sweetness of the Shabbat table and the beauty of Jewish family dynamics. Parents should bring their children to synagogue themselves and involve them in Jewish life wherever possible. We must encourage our children to lead the prayers and the public Torah readings where possible, such as reading Maftir. By raising our children with the proper Torah values, we ensure the continuity of the Jewish people for generations to come.

פרשת בהר

Parashat Behar

Shemita: A Lesson in Empathy

דַּבֵּר אֶל־בְּנֵי יִשְׂרָאֵל וְאָמַרְתָּ אֲלֵהֶם כִּי תָבֹאוּ אֶל הָאָרֶץ אֲשֶׁר אֲנִי נֹתֵן לָכֶם וְשָׁבְתָה הָאָרֶץ שַׁבָּת לַה׳:

"Speak to the Jewish people and say to them: When you enter the land that I assign to you, the land shall observe a sabbath of Hashem." [115]

This week's Parasha introduces us to one of the mitzvot which applies in the land of Israel, the mitzvah of Shemita. Shemita mirrors the Shabbat day of rest, by commanding us to observe a Shabbat of the land. Just as we refrain from working on Shabbat, Hashem commands us to rest our fields every seventh year. What is the purpose of this obligation? While various reasons exist to explain this mitzvah, Rabbenu Baḥya[116] offers a unique explanation. He suggests that Shemita allows wealthy individuals to experience

---

[115] Vayikra 25:2
[116] Rabbenu Baḥya Al Hatorah Shemot 21:2

poverty by not being able to work for one year every seven years. This way, every person will empathize with the plight of those who are less fortunate and not always able to find work. Our Parasha's repeated comparisons between the rich and the poor, says Rabbenu Baḥya, aims to cultivate awareness and sensitivity towards those who struggle. This, in turn, will motivate everyone to tend to the needs of those individuals and to assist them meaningfully.

Rav Ben-Haim told a story of Rav Yitzḥak of Volozhin which illustrates this point. During a harsh winter, Rav Yitzḥak visited a wealthy individual to collect tzedakah. The man invited the rabbi to come inside his house to speak, but Rav Yitzḥak insisted on standing outside in the cold for another minute. After a few minutes of talking, the wealthy man requested again for the rabbi to come inside and continue the conversation inside his house. Again, Rav Yitzḥak deflected his request and asked for a few more minutes outside. After a few more minutes the wealthy man begged the rabbi to please come inside, as they were both shivering from the cold. Rav Yitzḥak finally agreed to come in. After Rav Yitzḥak came into the house, he explained: "I wanted you to experience the discomfort of what it is like for a poor person to be outside in the frigid cold. When one lives in comfort, he cannot truly understand the pain and needs of those less fortunate." The rabbi wanted to teach the man how to empathize with the needs of those who struggle, and to encourage meaningful action to help them.

Many of us nowadays live relatively comfortable lifestyles where most of our basic necessities are met. However, we must never forget those who are less fortunate and are facing challenges that we may not fully comprehend. We are called by the Torah to provide financial and emotional support to those who are struggling, to show sensitivity to their needs and actively seek ways to assist them. A

Jew cannot solely live for himself in this world. We must work to develop our empathy so that we can alleviate the struggles of those less fortunate.

פרשת בחקתי

Parashat Beḥukotai

The Blessing of Enough

וְהִשִּׂיג לָכֶם דַּיִשׁ אֶת בָּצִיר וּבָצִיר יַשִּׂיג אֶת זֶרַע וַאֲכַלְתֶּם לַחְמְכֶם לָשֹׂבַע וִישַׁבְתֶּם
לָבֶטַח בְּאַרְצְכֶם:

"Your threshing shall overtake the vintage, and your vintage shall overtake the sowing; you shall eat your bread to satisfaction and dwell securely in your land."[117]

Parashat Beḥukotai presents the starkest of contrasts: abundant blessings that are promised to us when we keep the commandments of the Torah, followed by curses for disregarding the commandments of the Torah. One of the blessings promised when we keep the commandments is that we will eat our food and be satisfied. Rashi[118] explains this blessing to mean that we will be able to eat even a small portion of food and to be satiated from it. When blessed by Hashem, one can find contentment even with having

---

[117] Vayikra 26:5
[118] Rashi Vayikra 26:5

moderate portions. A genuine sense of satisfaction becomes priority over endless pursuits of more pleasure. This is the ultimate blessing the Torah can give.

Achieving this level of satisfaction does not exclusively depend on the blessing of Hashem. We ourselves must actively cultivate healthy habits, including mindful eating. Unfortunately, it has become common for people to overindulge at different social events where food is served. Overconsumption is a grave mistake that is detrimental to a person's health. Rambam, speaking both as a rabbi and as a world-renown physician, writes the following: "Overeating is like poison to anyone's body. It is the main source of all illness. Most illnesses which afflict a man are caused either by harmful foods or by his filling his belly and overeating even healthy foods." [119] Even eating the healthiest of foods can be harmful in excess. We must appreciate the wisdom of Rambam and adhere to his guidance to regulate our food intake.

In his book Moreh Nevuchim,[120] Rambam cites the verse in Mishle[121] that states that people often blame Hashem for their illnesses and then question Hashem's justice when they have problems in life. However, Rambam argues, it very often happens that people cause their own life problems by neglecting a healthy lifestyle both mentally and physically. When a person has difficulties in life, it is not always because of Hashem. Sometimes, it is a person's own fault, and the blame lies squarely on his own shoulders. Hashem gave us the responsibility of caring for ourselves and doing all that we can to be healthy.

---

[119] Halachot Deot 4:14
[120] Moreh Nevuchim 3:12
[121] Mishle 19:3

Rambam[122] beautifully states: "part of following the ways of Hashem is for a person to maintain his health." When a person exercises and avoids overeating by eating the right foods in the right quantities, his body functions in a healthy manner. This way, a person will be able to maximize his ability to serve Hashem properly. One of the beauties of Judaism is that the Torah gives us the ability to sanctify even the most mundane activities. Maintaining a healthy diet and body is in fact an act of service to Hashem. We must care for ourselves and encourage our loved ones not to eat unnecessarily and or overindulge in food intake. The true blessing is not necessarily to have abundance in life, but to find the healthy balance where we can have a small amount and be content with what we have. May we always be inspired by the Torah to lead the healthiest lifestyles that we can, and thus merit that Hashem bless us with good health and contentment.

---

[122] Halachot Deot 4:1

Penine Ḥaim

BEMIDBAR

Penine Ḥaim

פרשת במדבר

Parashat Bemidbar

Counting for Blessing

שְׂאוּ אֶת רֹאשׁ כָּל עֲדַת בְּנֵי יִשְׂרָאֵל לְמִשְׁפְּחֹתָם לְבֵית אֲבֹתָם בְּמִסְפַּר שֵׁמוֹת כָּל זָכָר לְגֻלְגְּלֹתָם :

"Take a census of the whole Jewish nation by the families of its ancestral houses, listing the names, every male, head by head."[123]

The book of Bemidbar begins with Hashem commanding Moshe to take a census of the Jewish people in the desert. Rashi[124] explains that Hashem counts the Jews several times in the Torah as a way of showing His deep affection for His children the same way a person one regularly counts things that are precious to him. In the same way, Hashem's children are dear to Him and He regularly counts them.

---

[123] Bemidbar 1:2
[124] Rashi Bemidbar 1:1

The Gemara[125] teaches us that to count Jews by head is prohibited. When people are counted individually, each person is scrutinized and can be brought to judgement (Ayin Hara – the "evil eye"). So how were the Jewish people counted? The answer is that they were counted using a mitzvah, a donation to the Mishkan. Each person donated half a shekel as tzedakah to the uptake of the Mishkan. These donations were counted, and that way they could take a census of how many Jews there were. The Mekubalim[126] explain that the evil eye does not have power over things that are related to a mitzvah. The coins that were used as donations to the Temple were being used for a mitzvah purpose; therefore, the Jews being counted were immune to the negative judgments that can be caused by Ayin Hara.

This offers us an invaluable lesson: when our resources and interests are dedicated for the service of Hashem, we make ourselves immune to Ayin Hara. By consistently directing our finances towards spiritual endeavors and helping others, we need not be worried about being scrutinized for specific behaviors. However, if we view wealth as a means of superficially holding ourselves higher than others, this can unfortunately attract negative spiritual judgment that impacts ourselves and our families. Blessings that we receive from Hashem should never be misused in this way. Instead, when our wealth is being used not to flaunt ourselves and seek fame, but rather to elevate our spiritual lives to glorify Hashem's name, no harm can befall us. When we live modestly and dedicate our efforts and resources to contribute positively to the world at large, we can live securely, and rest assured that the negative judgements of Ayin Hara will not affect us.

---

[125] Yoma 22b
[126] See Pele Yoetz Ayin Hara

פרשת נשא

Parashat Naso

A Deeper Look at Birkat Kohanim

דַּבֵּר אֶל אַהֲרֹן וְאֶל בָּנָיו לֵאמֹר כֹּה תְבָרְכוּ אֶת בְּנֵי יִשְׂרָאֵל אָמוֹר לָהֶם : יְבָרֶכְךָ ה'
וְיִשְׁמְרֶךָ :

"Speak to Aharon and his sons: Thus shall you bless the people of Israel. Say to them: 'May Hashem bless you and protect you.'"[127]

Parashat Naso features one of the most well-known blessings in the Torah - Birkat Kohanim, the daily blessing recited by Kohanim for the Jewish people. The blessing starts, "*Yevarechecha Hashem Veyishmerecha,*" meaning "May Hashem bless you and protect you."

Rashi[128] quotes the Midrash which explains that "*Yevarechecha*" means that Hashem should bless us with financial wealth, while "*Veyishmerecha*" means Hashem should protect us so that bandits do not steal the money that we were blessed with. In other words,

---

[127] Bemidbar 6:23
[128] Rashi Bemidbar 6:24 quoting Midrash Tanḥuma Naso 10

Hashem will bless us that the prosperity that should remain with us and not be stolen away.

The meaning of the Midrash's interpretation can extend far deeper than their literal sense. There are many types of "bandits" who can strip away our blessings. For example, these "bandits" can also symbolically refer to our inner bandit - the *yetzer hara*, or evil inclination. The blessing of the Kohanim is also that Hashem protect us from our own *yetzer hara*, so that our *yetzer hara* should not "steal" Hashem's gifts from us by causing us to waste them. Similarly, the Kohanim's blessing is also that the wealth we are blessed with should not corrupt our hearts by making us materialistic and by making money the primary focus of our lives. The Kohanim's blessing, therefore, encompasses that we should be able to make wise choices with the blessings Hashem gives us, using them in the right manner that aligns with our values and brings us happiness.

There are many people whose personalities unfortunately change after acquiring wealth, causing them to become arrogant and self-centered. Arrogance contradicts the blessing that Hashem has given. An individual whose financial wealth causes him to become arrogant may be better off not receiving the wealth in the first place. We should always remember that wealth can sometimes be sent as a punishment to a person. In the book of Kohelet, [129] Shelomo Hamelech writes that at times, "Riches are kept for its owner for his own hurt." In other words, it sometimes happens that individuals receive wealth as a punishment to hurt them. Instead of bringing joy to a person, this type of wealth ends up being spent on unnecessary bills and on alleviating the undue stress created from poor decision-making that was made by the recipient of the wealth. This type of

---

[129] Kohelet 5:12

wealth is reserved to hurt them and not a blessing at all. In such scenarios, those who are given this type of wealth will eventually come to remember how their quality of life was much better before they were given the wealth. After the wealth ruins their lives, they come to wish that they never had it in the first place.

Therefore, we must pray to Hashem every day that all our income should only come as a blessing for us, for all areas of our lives. We must appreciate the blessings that Hashem has granted us and use them as a call to action: to bring more Torah, more kindness, more goodness, and more peace to the world. May it be Hashem's will that all the prosperity we are given should only be a source of comfort, health, peace, and blessing for our lives and for our families.

פרשת בהעלתך

Parashat Behaalotecha

Lessons from Miriam and Aharon on Avoiding Lashon Hara

וַתְּדַבֵּר מִרְיָם וְאַהֲרֹן בְּמֹשֶׁה עַל אֹדוֹת הָאִשָּׁה הַכֻּשִׁית אֲשֶׁר לָקָח כִּי אִשָּׁה כֻשִׁית לָקָח: וַיֹּאמְרוּ הֲרַק אַךְ בְּמֹשֶׁה דִּבֶּר ה' הֲלֹא גַּם בָּנוּ דִבֵּר וַיִּשְׁמַע ה' :

"Miriam and Aharon spoke against Moshe because of the Cushite woman he had taken [as his wife]: They said 'Has Hashem only spoken only through Moshe? Has [Hashem] not spoken through us as well?' And Hashem heard."[130]

This week's Parasha presents a unique and thought-provoking episode. The Parasha records that Aharon and Miriam, both prophets themselves, spoke Lashon Hara (slander) about their brother Moshe. What was their conversation about? Rashi[131] explains that they were upset that their brother Moshe separated from his wife so that he could receive prophecy. Miriam felt that it

---

[130] Bemidbar 12:1-2
[131] Rashi Bemidbar 12:1-2

was inappropriate for Moshe to separate from his wife just so he can receive prophecy; after all, Aharon and Miriam were also both prophets and received prophecy from Hashem, but they were able to remain married and not separate from their spouses. Why did Moshe consider himself different from other prophets in needing to separate from his wife?

In essence, Miriam and Aharon were correct; however, they did not realize that Moshe was a prophet on a different level from them. Moshe had to be ready for prophecy at any moment and therefore it was necessary for him to abstain from his wife.

The Midrash[132] points out that Miriam's Lashon Hara was one of the mildest types of Lashon Hara possible. Miriam had positive intentions in speaking about Moshe, since she wanted to help Moshe change his "mistake" and resume intimacy with his wife. Nonetheless, she was still punished for her speech against Moshe. Rambam[133] takes this idea several steps further in highlighting how mild Miriam's Lashon Hara really was. Rambam notes that Miriam obviously did not intend to hurt Moshe with her Lashon Hara. As Moshe's older sister, she put herself in danger earlier in her life to watch over him by the river when he was a baby. She took so much care of him and helped raise him. She certainly loved Moshe and did not want to hurt him. Furthermore, she did not actually speak negatively about Moshe Rabbenu; she only equated him to being on the same level as other prophets. Furthermore, the Torah notes that Moshe Rabbenu was the humblest of all men and would not be offended by the Lashon Hara. Although all this was the case, Miriam was still punished harshly for speaking in such a manner about Moshe. This serves as a powerful reminder: if Hashem did not

---

[132] Devarim Rabba 6
[133] Halachot Tumat Tzaraat 16:10

forgive even the mildest form of Lashon Hara that Miriam said, how much more careful must we be in guarding our speech?

A practical rule of thumb to guide us in whether something is considered Lashon Hara or not is to consider if we would feel comfortable saying the same thing directly in front of the person we are talking about. If we would say the same words, in the same manner, with the same intonations, in their actual presence, it is most likely not Lashon Hara. On the other hand, if we would not say the same words in their presence, it most likely is Lashon Hara. The Gemara[134] notes that Rabbi Yose exemplified this approach to Lashon Hara: he never said something about his fellow that he had to look back to see if he was there or not. Rabbi Yose used this measure to identify if his speech was ever Lashon Hara or not. Especially in social settings or Shabbat gatherings, where opinions and judgements of other people are easily shared, we must refrain from participating in Lashon Hara. We must keep in mind that even words spoken with good intentions can sometimes cause unintended consequences. Let our speech always be used for the positive, for studying Torah, for fulfilling mitzvot, and for helping people.

---

[134] Shabbat 118b

פרשת שלח

Parashat Shelaḥ

Embracing Emuna in the Face of Doubt

שְׁלַח לְךָ אֲנָשִׁים וְיָתֻרוּ אֶת אֶרֶץ כְּנַעַן אֲשֶׁר אֲנִי נֹתֵן לִבְנֵי יִשְׂרָאֵל אִישׁ אֶחָד אִישׁ אֶחָד לְמַטֵּה אֲבֹתָיו תִּשְׁלָחוּ כֹּל נָשִׂיא בָהֶם :

"Send agents to scout the land of Canaan, which I am giving to the Jewish people; send one participant from each of their ancestral tribes, each one a chieftain among them."[135]

The incident of the spies is one of the most enlightening passages in the Torah. The Jewish people were preparing to enter the land of Israel that Hashem promised to our forefathers. However, instead of entering the land with confidence and joy, they did just the opposite. Rashi[136] cites the Gemara which explains that the idea of sending spies to Israel did not originate from Hashem; rather, it started with the Jews demanding that spies be sent to investigate the land. Hashem said to Moshe, "Send [the spies] at your own will and

---

[135] Bemidbar 13:1
[136] Rashi Bemidbar 13:1 quoting Sota 34b

discretion, but not at My will and discretion." Hashem allowed Moshe to send spies to alleviate the Jewish people's lack of faith. However, Hashem disapproved of the decision to investigate the land.

One key lesson from this Parasha is the importance of Emuna and unwavering trust in Hashem. When Hashem commands us to do something, we must have the strength to proceed without fear. The Torah[137] teaches, "be wholehearted with Hashem, your God." This means avoiding doubt or over-analyzing Hashem's directives. When Hashem gives us a mitzvah, we should be prepared to follow through without hesitation.

The famous rabbi and philosopher Rabbenu Baḥya [138] teaches a profound truth: "One of the great principles of being cautious in life is not to be too cautious." In other words, excessive caution and fear can sometimes paralyze us. This was crucial mistake of the Jewish people in our Parasha. Instead of trusting Hashem that the land of Israel would be good, they demanded that spies should investigate it with their limited intellect, essentially deciding for themselves whether this venture would worthwhile or not. As the verse in Kohelet[139] says: "Do not be overly righteous and don't over-analyze, why should you be left desolate?"

This principle can be applied in other areas as well. Often, overthinking and over-analyzing can be detrimental. For example, when it comes to getting married, parents or children may believe that more investigation will lead to better outcomes, but very often, the opposite occurs. Those who spend too much time considering all their options will often struggle to find a spouse and ultimately miss

---

[137] Devarim 18:13
[138] Intro to Ḥovot Halevavot
[139] Kohelet 7:16

out. It often happens that those who approach the process with more simplicity are the ones who find their match and experience greater happiness. We must strive to serve Hashem with simplicity and genuine faith. Doing so will remove unnecessary stress and allow us to live life with more meaning and joy.

פרשת קרח

Parashat Koraḥ

When Unity Trumps Mercy

אִם כְּמוֹת כָּל הָאָדָם יְמֻתוּן אֵלֶּה וּפְקֻדַּת כָּל הָאָדָם יִפָּקֵד עֲלֵיהֶם לֹא ה' שְׁלָחָנִי:

"If these men die as all men die and the fate of all men will be visited upon them, then Hashem has not sent me."[140]

This week's Parasha tells us the story of Koraḥ - the instigator of the strongest rebellion against Moshe and Aharon. When we pay close attention to the text, we find Moshe acting out of character. Until now, every time there was a complaint or rebellion against Hashem, Moshe would fall on his face and pray to Hashem. This was the case by the rebellion regarding the lack of meat in Parashat Behaalotecha and by the incident of the spies who slandered against Israel in Parashat Shelaḥ. Suddenly, when it comes to dealing with Koraḥ, we find Moshe asserting himself strongly and confronting this rebellion in a very intense and exceptionally harsh manner. Moshe even made an ultimatum: "If these people's death is that of all

---

[140] Bemidbar 16:29

humankind, if their lot is humankind's common fate, it was not Hashem who sent me." In other words, Moshe effectively said, if the people of Koraḥ would die a normal death, the Jews could consider him a false prophet. Only if they would die an extraordinary death where they would be swallowed by the ground would it then prove that Moshe is a true prophet of Hashem. Immediately after Moshe finished making this declaration, the ground opened and swallowed Koraḥ alive with all his possessions. They indeed died an extraordinary and unnatural death.

The question arises: why is Moshe's reaction so harsh in this episode? The question is even more bothersome when we consider that Koraḥ was Moshe's cousin. He was family. Moshe did not seem to have any mercy on these individuals after they refused to listen, even though they were his own family. Why was such a strong reaction necessary?

Moshe's harsh response to Koraḥ stemmed from recognizing the tremendous danger Koraḥ posed to the Jewish nation. Koraḥ, a savvy politician, portrayed himself as a pious person who cared about the entire nation. He deceptively proclaimed publicly, "all the Jewish nation are holy! All should be able to lead and serve!" This facade masked Koraḥ's true desire: personal power and prestige. The Talmud Yerushalmi[141] states that Koraḥ would openly mock Moshe and Aharon by ridiculing halachot that were seemingly illogical. For example, Koraḥ would ask them, "Does a room full of Torah scrolls need a Mezuzah? Does a Tallit made completely of Techelet require Techelet strings?" These were not genuine questions. Koraḥ was only using these questions as a tool to manipulate the Torah, advance his own personal agenda and sow discord within the Jewish people.

---

[141] Yerushalmi Sanhedrin 10:1

Moshe saw right through Koraḥ's rebellion, understanding that the rebellion was not about helping the nation, but about Koraḥ's personal interests and desire for power. Koraḥ craved the priesthood only for himself and used his arguments to drive a wedge between the Jewish people and their leader. Moshe foresaw that the Jewish nation would fall apart due to Koraḥ's deception. Koraḥ was a threat to the existence of the Jewish nation. When Koraḥ and his followers stubbornly refused to even meet Moshe Rabbenu, reconciliation was impossible. The only way to preserve the future of the Jewish nation was in danger was with a harsh response. Eliminating Koraḥ and his ideology by Hashem became the only viable option to end the discord.

The lesson we must all learn is to never twist the Torah as a means towards personal gain. We must understand the danger of personal interests causing discord among the Jewish people. When we observe the Torah, our aim should always be to sanctify Hashem's name, to do what is best for our nation, and to foster peace in the world.

פרשת חקת

Parashat Ḥukkat

Controlling Anger for a More Harmonious Life

וַיַּקְהִלוּ מֹשֶׁה וְאַהֲרֹן אֶת הַקָּהָל אֶל פְּנֵי הַסֶּלַע וַיֹּאמֶר לָהֶם שִׁמְעוּ נָא הַמֹּרִים הֲמִן הַסֶּלַע הַזֶּה נוֹצִיא לָכֶם מָיִם:

"Moshe and Aharon assembled the congregation in front of the rock; and he said to them, 'Listen, you rebels, shall we get water for you out of this rock?'"[142]

This Parasha presents one of the most painful and troublesome questions of the Torah: Why was Moshe Rabbenu denied entry into the land of Israel? Moshe was perhaps the greatest leader in the history of our nation. He devoted his life to taking us out of slavery, bringing us the Torah at Har Sinai, and praying on behalf of our nation time after time. His sole dream was to complete his mission of leading the nation into the Promised Land. If there was ever one person who deserved to reach his goals, that man was Moshe Rabbenu. Yet, in our parasha, Hashem delivers judgement that

---

[142] Bemidbar 20:10

Moshe will pass away in the desert and will not lead the nation into Israel, because he hit the rock and did not sanctify Hashem's name at Kaddesh. What exactly was Moshe's sin?

This topic puzzles even the greatest commentators on the Torah. One of the enlightening explanations of Moshe's sin is Rambam's explanation. Rambam[143] explains that Moshe's mistake was his anger. The Jewish people were not wrong for their frustrations at the time: they were in a hot desert; they were thirsty and there was a lack of water. However, Moshe's reaction to their frustrations lacked sensitivity. Moshe reacted angrily and called them "rebels." This expression of anger, says the Rambam, was the mistake that sealed Moshe Rabbenu's fate. Although this small expression of anger seemed to be a small mistake, it resulted in a strong punishment since Hashem holds leaders to a higher standard. Leaders serve as role models for the nation, and any slight misstep carries the potential to mislead others. For this reason, Moshe's mistake of getting angry resulted in him being denied permission to enter Eretz Yisrael.

The Torah here teaches that we must be extremely careful to avoid the trait of anger. Anger can warp our judgment, leading us to say and do things that one would never do otherwise. The Gemara[144] teaches, "Any man who grows angry; if he is a prophet, his prophecy is removed from him; if he is a wise man, his wisdom is removed from him." Arizal[145] goes even further, saying that the sin of getting angry is worse than any sin in the Torah. When one gets angry, Arizal says, his holy soul is taken away from him and is replaced by an animalistic soul which plunges a person down to a very low

143 Rambam Introduction to Pirke Avot Chapter 4
144 Pesaḥim 66b
145 Shaar Ruaḥ Hakodesh 5748 Yerushalayim edition, page 33 D"H *Gam Midat Hakaas*

spiritual state. Rav Ḥaim Vital writes that his teacher, Arizal, was extremely scrupulous to avoid the trait of anger more than any other prohibition due to the devastating impact it has on a person's spiritual well-being.

The consequences of unchecked anger are tragically evident in everyday life. Rav Ben-Haim recounts that he has seen marriages shattered due to one petty, but explosive, episode between a husband and wife. He has seen siblings estranged for many years because of one angry argument between the family members. In one episode, Rav Ben-Haim recalled that a woman once told him that when she and her husband got into an explosive argument, her husband took the picture of her parents, tore the picture in half and flushed it down the toilet. In anger, a person can descend to low levels that would be unimaginable even to himself. In a state of anger, we lose our rational thinking and cannot see things in an objective and clear way. Anger ultimately tears apart lives and relationships.

Although Moshe Rabbenu did not descend to such extreme levels, for a person of his great stature, even a minor lack of patience was enough for Hashem to issue a consequence. The lesson is clear: we must put forward our utmost effort to control our anger and avoid our triggers. By doing so, we cultivate clarity, peace of mind, and the ability to navigate life's challenges in the most graceful manner possible. We must remember that sometimes, even the slightest flicker of anger can have far-reaching consequences. Let us heed the wisdom of the Torah and strive to live with greater self-awareness and emotional control, and this way we can create a more harmonious world for ourselves and for those around us.

פרשת בלק

Parashat Balak

Embracing Our Heritage

כִּי מֵרֹאשׁ צֻרִים אֶרְאֶנּוּ וּמִגְּבָעוֹת אֲשׁוּרֶנּוּ הֶן עָם לְבָדָד יִשְׁכֹּן וּבַגּוֹיִם לֹא
יִתְחַשָּׁב:

"As I see them from the mountain tops and gaze on them from the heights, there is a nation that dwells apart, not reckoned among the nations."[146]

Our Parasha features the story of the wicked prophet Bilaam, who attempted to curse the Jewish nation. Hashem blocked all of Bilaam's attempts by turning his curses into blessings. A question may be asked about Bilaam. Why did the Jewish nation have to be concerned about Bilaam's curses in the first place? It is known that Bilaam was an immoral and wicked person. The Gemara[147] notes that Bilaam was immoral to the point that he had marital relations

---

[146] Bemidbar 23:9
[147] Sanhedrin 105b

with his own donkey. How could a wicked man's curses carry any impact at all?

The answer lies in timing. The Gemara[148] explains that Bilaam was able to determine the moment that Hashem would get angry, so to speak, and judge the Jews for their sins. He planned to curse the Jews at that specific moment of judgment and vulnerability. At such moments of weakness, he could successfully bring harm to the Jews. In Hashem's kindness, He did not judge the Jews during those times, thus leaving Bilaam's curses powerless.

Although he was unsuccessful with his curses, Bilaam discovered a more potent weapon: assimilation. Bilaam understood that enticing the Jews to intermingle with the Moabite women would cause them to lose their sanctity and lead to their downfall. Sadly, this last tactic had tragic consequences. When the Jews assimilated and intermingled with the Moabite women, a plague struck, killing twenty-four thousand Jews. Bilaam recognized that Jewish sanctity is the secret to our success. As soon as the Jews would assimilate with the Moabites, they would become vulnerable. There is an amazing lesson we learn from this Parasha. As long as we keep our sanctity as the Jewish nation, Hashem protects us from all threats, and we have nothing to fear. We are only vulnerable when we lose our sanctity.

Assimilation still remains a significant threat to the existence of Jewish people today. Before the Holocaust, the world Jewish population was around 17 million Jews. After the Holocaust, by the year 1945, the world Jewish population was around 11 million. Seventy-five years later, in the year 2020, the total Jewish population around the world stands at approximately 17 million, meaning that our population may or may not have recovered to its

---

[148] Berachot 7a, Sanhedrin 105b

pre-Holocaust level.[149] In comparison, the world human population from 1945 to 2020 more than tripled (2.3 billion to 7.8 billion). The world Jewish population grew at a much slower rate than the rest of the world. This disparity highlights the problem of assimilation and intermarriage. If the Jewish population would grow at the same rate as the rest of the world population, there could be over 35 million Jews today after the Holocaust, not 17 million. Assimilation is a silent Holocaust that hinders our population growth and remains a threat to our nation to this day.

Rav Ben-Haim shared a personal story of a wealthy man who dreamed of his children becoming doctors. He invested heavily in their secular education but neglected their Jewish education. Years later, Rav Ben-Haim visited the man when he was on his deathbed. The man cried to him and shared his fear that his children would not care to give him a Jewish burial or even say Kaddish for him, because they were unaffiliated and disconnected from their Jewish heritage. This story emphasizes the urgent need to recognize and address the threats of assimilation. The most important investment we can make is in our children's Jewish education. Preserving our sanctity ensures that Hashem should bless our nation to grow spiritually as well as to grow physically in our population numbers.

---

[149] Pew Research Center Study, Jewish Americans in 2020. https://www.pewresearch.org/religion/2021/05/11/the-size-of-the-u-s-jewish-population/#is-the-jewish-share-of-the-u-s-population-stable-growing-or-shrinking

פרשת פינחס

Parashat Pineḥas

The Power of Baal Pe'or

כִּי צֹרְרִים הֵם לָכֶם בְּנִכְלֵיהֶם אֲשֶׁר נִכְּלוּ לָכֶם עַל דְּבַר פְּעוֹר וְעַל דְּבַר כָּזְבִּי בַת
נְשִׂיא מִדְיָן אֲחֹתָם הַמֻּכָּה בְיוֹם הַמַּגֵּפָה עַל דְּבַר פְּעוֹר:

"For they antagonized you through their conspiracy over the matter of Pe'or, and over the matter of Kozbi, the daughter of the prince of Midian their sister, who was slain on the day of the plague due to the matter of Pe'or."[150]

At the end of last week's parasha, the Jewish nation worshipped Baal Pe'or, a local deity worshipped by the Moabites. Together with the sin of sexually immoral behavior, this idolatry triggered a devastating plague that claimed the lives of 24,000 Jews. Only Pineḥas's decisive intervention, slaying leader of the tribe Shimon, stopped the further spread of the plague.

---

[150] Bemidbar 25:18

The question can be asked: what made the Jews so attached to worship of Baal Pe'or? The Gemara[151] describes the worship of this deity: the worshippers would eat laxative foods and would then defecate before the idol. One story in the Gemara even depicts a Jewish man who wanted to mock Baal Pe'or. He not only defecated before the idol, but he also went ahead and wiped himself with the idol's nose. The priests of the idol not only did not rebuke him, but they also praised him and remarked, "there was never a man who worshipped our idol in such an excellent manner!" This type of behavior is obviously repulsive to any person. How could anyone become drawn to such repulsive practices?

Rav Ḥaim Shmuelevitz[152] offers a profound explanation. Baal Pe'or represented the seductive idea that no behavior is too disgusting or immoral. In general, other forms of idol worship held by certain moral codes. One who would disrespect their deity or their worship would be ostracized. Baal Pe'or, however, abolished all boundaries. Even the act of defecation, universally considered a repulsive act, was considered a pleasing act to Baal Pe'or.

This lawlessness offered by Baal Pe'or with no rules, boundaries, or moral standards held a dangerous allure. This ideology, which remains a danger nowadays, promotes the idea that humans are above any laws, guidelines, or moral compass. In fact, any type of behavior can be desirable if it fulfills human desires. This ideology ultimately leads to the moral collapse of an entire society.

On the other hand, the same concept of human potential can also inspire us to serve Hashem. The Torah affirms human greatness; we are created in the image of God.[153] Yet instead of leading us to break

---

[151] Sanhedrin 64a
[152] Siḥot Mussar Year 5732, Article #34, "Baal Pe'or"
[153] Bereshit 1:27

moral boundaries, this greatness underscores the immense responsibility on our shoulders. The greater we are, the more we must strive to emulate Hashem's will as expressed in the Torah. By harnessing our potential and using it to embrace moral responsibility, we can transform this ideology into a great force for good in the world.

פרשת מטות

Parashat Mattot

Beyond Oaths: The Power of Our Words

אִישׁ כִּי יִדֹּר נֶדֶר לַה' אוֹ הִשָּׁבַע שְׁבֻעָה לֶאְסֹר אִסָּר עַל נַפְשׁוֹ לֹא יַחֵל דְּבָרוֹ כְּכָל
הַיֹּצֵא מִפִּיו יַעֲשֶׂה:

"If a man makes a vow to Hashem or takes an oath imposing an obligation on himself, he shall not desecrate his word; he must carry out all that has crossed his lips."[154]

This week's Parasha delves into the power and responsibility of our words, specifically through the concept of oaths. According to Jewish law, making an oath to do or not to do something becomes a binding commitment. Similarly, a person can make an item forbidden to himself by swearing that he will not benefit from the item. The Torah states that one may not desecrate his word. This teaches us that we much treat our words as having sanctity.

---

[154] Bemidbar 30:3

Taking our oaths lightly is a serious offense. Rambam[155] rules that swearing falsely or unnecessarily is one of the gravest sins which requires atonement on par with a capital offense. Sadly, many people disregard the severity of false or unnecessary oaths. In business, for example, it often happens that people swear unnecessarily to convince others to do what they would like. Sometimes, individuals will event go so far to swear by the life of their parents or other family members or will swear by the Torah or even by the sacred name of Hashem over the most trivial matters *ḥas veshalom*. Even if a person intends to keep his word, swearing without reason can carry difficult consequences. The Gemara[156] teaches that due to the sin of oaths and vows, one's children can be taken from this world, Heaven forbid.

The Gemara[157] recounts the following story regarding vows and oaths: there once was a widow who was entrusted with a gold coin to watch over. To keep it safe, she stored the gold coin in her sack of flour. One day, she accidentally baked the coin into a loaf of bread which she then went and distributed to the poor. When defending herself for losing the coin, the widow swore on the life of her child that she didn't derive benefit from the coin in any way. Soon after, her child died. The rabbis explained that although her oath was mostly true and she intended it to be true, her words also contained a slight falsehood. The woman did, in fact, derive some benefit from the coin. By baking the coin inside the dough, she gained a small benefit by saving a small amount of flour which would have gone into the loaf of bread. Even though her error was slight, her oath was indeed false, and she was held accountable for swearing on the life

---

[155] Halachot Teshuva 1:2
[156] Shabbat 32b
[157] Gittin 35a

of her child. This powerful story teaches us about the power of our words. Even when we think we are telling the truth, sometimes there might be a mistake or slight falsehood that we do not recognize. Therefore, swearing even truthfully should be avoided unless it is absolutely necessary.

A refined person can be recognized by how carefully he uses his or her words. Recognizing the power of our speech, we should strive for honesty even without making an oath or swear. That way, our words will carry true weight even without taking an oath and can serve positive purposes throughout our lives.

פרשת מסעי

Parashat Mas'e

From Punishment to Growth: A Vision for Rehabilitation

לִבְנֵי יִשְׂרָאֵל וְלַגֵּר וְלַתּוֹשָׁב בְּתוֹכָם תִּהְיֶינָה שֵׁשׁ הֶעָרִים הָאֵלֶּה לְמִקְלָט לָנוּס
שָׁמָּה כָּל מַכֵּה נֶפֶשׁ בִּשְׁגָגָה:

*"These six cities shall serve the Jews and the resident aliens among
them for refuge, so that any man who slays a person unintentionally
may flee there."*[158]

This week's Parasha introduces us to the concept of cities of refuge.
In ancient Israel, if someone unintentionally killed another person,
the family members of the victim held the right of vengeance – they
could kill the unintentional murderer. At the same time, the
unintentional murderer had the right to flee a designated city of the
Leviim for protection. Once within the city, the family members
could no longer harm him. Forty-eight cities of Leviim were
designated by Hashem to serve as spiritual centers for the land of

---

[158] Bemidbar 35:15

Israel.[159] The Leviim were a tribe solely dedicated to the service of Hashem through Torah study and spiritual endeavors. It was in these locations that unintentional killers sought refuge.

The question can be asked, why do unintentional killers have to flee to these cities? Wouldn't imprisonment perhaps be a better solution, like many modern criminal correctional systems?

The simple answer is no. The Torah and our rabbis do not advocate for imprisonment as a means for correction. The closest example resembling imprisonment in the Torah involved the wood gatherer on Shabbat,[160] who was kept in a temporary detention center while his punishment was being decided by Moshe Rabbenu. This detention center was not a punishment but rather a temporary holding measure until a sentence would be issued.

Jail time is a punishment that the Torah does not suggest for crime since it does not encourage corrective action. It only temporarily prevents more criminal activity from being done. This is in stark contrast to the Torah's mandate for the perpetrator to run to the Levite city of refuge. Due to the positive atmosphere of the Levite city, the perpetrators will be encouraged to reflect internally and be influenced by the character and spiritual guidance of the Leviim. The spiritual environment of the Levite city will naturally encourage positive growth and for the negligent perpetrator to live a life according to the Torah's values. The Gemara[161] teaches us that when a student goes to exile, his rabbis must accompany him. The rabbi must follow him to exile since the rabbi's guidance is essential to his spiritual growth and reintegration into society.

---

[159] Rambam Halachot Rotzeaḥ 8:9
[160] Bemidbar 15:32
[161] Makkot 10a

This is a crucial idea for parents and educators. When responding to negative behavior, we must make sure not to respond merely by preventing its occurrence again. Rather we must aim to place a child in an environment where they have the potential to grow and thrive, with positive influence from their surroundings. David Hamelech writes in Tehillim:[162] "Distance yourself from evil and do good." Distancing from evil does not suffice; one must also replace it with corrective positive action. This will allow for long-lasting change which will enable communities and societies to flourish.

---

[162] Tehillim 34:15

Penine Ḥaim

DEVARIM

פרשת דברים

Parashat Devarim

The Power of Indirect Rebuke

אֵלֶּה הַדְּבָרִים אֲשֶׁר דִּבֶּר מֹשֶׁה אֶל כָּל יִשְׂרָאֵל בְּעֵבֶר הַיַּרְדֵּן בַּמִּדְבָּר בָּעֲרָבָה מוֹל סוּף בֵּין פָּארָן וּבֵין תֹּפֶל וְלָבָן וַחֲצֵרֹת וְדִי זָהָב :

"These are the words which Moshe spoke to all Israel on that side of the Jordan in the desert, in the plain opposite the Red Sea, between Paran and Tophel and Lavan and Ḥazerot and Di Zahav."[163]

Sefer Devarim, the fifth book of the Torah, serves as a review of the entire Torah and the commandments Hashem entrusted to the Jewish people throughout their journey. The book is also known as Mishneh Torah, the repetition of the Torah. In this book, Moshe narrates with Divine inspiration the past experiences of the Jews and the lessons that they hold. These messages were to guide them going forward as they would enter a new chapter until Yehoshua's leadership after Moshe would pass away.

---

[163] Devarim 1:1

The review begins with describing the stage: "In the desert, in the plain opposite the Red Sea, between Paran and Tofel and Lavan and Ḥazerot and Di Zahav." Intriguingly, some of these places do not seem to exist the Torah. For example, what exactly are "Lavan?" and "Di Zahav?" These locations are not mentioned anywhere else. Rashi[164] quotes the Midrash that explains that these locations were all veiled references to the Jews' past transgressions. For example, "opposite the Red Sea," is a reference to the complaints the Jews had before Hashem split the sea, when they questioned why Hashem took them out to the desert to die. "Di Zahav" is a hint to the Golden calf the Jews worshipped in the desert while Moshe was on Har Sinai [Zahav means gold in Hebrew]. These subtle allusions serve as gentle rebukes, urging the Jewish people to avoid making the same mistakes when they move forward under Yehoshua's leadership.

The question may be asked: why does Moshe use such an indirect approach when rebuking the Jews, by making unusual, veiled references to the locations where they sinned? Why doesn't Moshe simply deliver a more direct rebuke? The answer lies in the art of effective communication and rebuke. The book of Mishle[165] teaches: "The words of the wise are listened to when said pleasantly." Most often, blunt criticism triggers defense mechanisms, leading to rejection of the criticism. Whenever we are criticized directly, even when it comes from a very wise person, it is human nature to automatically reject. Pointing out faults directly is uncomfortable and is usually met with resistance as opposed to acceptance. Therefore, indirect rebuke but with a pleasant manner can often yield better results. By mentioning the places of their

[164] Rashi Devarim 1:1 quoting Sifre 1:1
[165] Mishle 9:17

transgressions indirectly, Moshe allowed the Jews to reflect and absorb his message without feeling that they were being attacked, in a way that preserved their respect.

This lesson resonates deeply in parenting. Instead of directly criticizing children's flaws, we should strive for indirect, positive guidance while preserving their dignity. If there is a suggestion that needs to be made, it can be done in a way that encourages self-reflection. A child will then be empowered to identify his weak points on his own and change them. Harsh and confrontational rebukes often backfire. Rather, we should build up those around us with encouragement and positivity.

פרשת ואתחנן

Parashat Va'etḥanan

Beyond Reward: Serving Hashem with Love

אֶעְבְּרָה נָּא וְאֶרְאֶה אֶת הָאָרֶץ הַטּוֹבָה אֲשֶׁר בְּעֵבֶר הַיַּרְדֵּן הָהָר הַטּוֹב הַזֶּה
וְהַלְּבָנוֹן:

"Please, let me cross over and see the good land that is on the other side of the Jordan, this good mountain and Lebanon."[166]

Our Parasha opens with Moshe's emotional plea to Hashem to enter the land of Israel. Hashem had decreed that, due to his earlier sin of hitting the rock, Moshe would not be allowed to enter the land of Israel. Nonetheless, Moshe's yearning was tremendous. The Midrash[167] states that Moshe pleaded with Hashem no less than five hundred fifteen times to enter the land of Israel!

What made Moshe so eager to enter the land of Israel? The Gemara[168] asks this question: "Did he desire the delicious fruits of Israel which made him long for the Land of Israel?" Obviously, this

---

[166] Devarim 3:25
[167] Devarim Rabbah 11:10
[168] Sota 14a

was not the case. Rather, the Gemara answers, Moshe wanted to enter the land of Israel to perform the mitzvot of the Torah which can only be fulfilled in the land of Israel and receive reward for performing them.

The question can be asked: it is certainly understandable that Moshe Rabbenu wanted to enter the land of Israel so that he can perform the mitzvot that can only be performed in the land. The Gemara, however, seems to highlight that Moshe wanted to receive reward for the mitzvot he would do in Israel. It is well-known that Pirke Avot[169] teaches us that we should not serve Hashem like servants who serve just to receive reward! The highest level of performing mitzvot is not for personal gain, but only out of the purest love for Hashem. If this is true, why does the Gemara highlight that Moshe Rabbenu wanted to receive reward for doing the mitzvot in Israel?

The answer can be understood by the following illustration: imagine a child coming home from school having received straight A's on his report card. The proud father rewards the child by buying him a $20 dollar gift. From the father's perspective, is the reward for his child the $20 gift that he bought? Obviously not. The ultimate reward, which has no value, is the child succeeding in school and setting himself on a good path for success in life. The father is delighted for the opportunity to buy a gift for his child to sweeten the experience of his child's great accomplishment.

In a similar vein, Hashem is our Father in Heaven and we are his children. Whenever we do good, Hashem is delighted [so to speak] to bless His children and reward us for our good deeds. By following His mitzvot, we give Hashem the "ability" to shower us with prosperity and blessing. Conversely, when we make the wrong choices, it "hurts" Hashem, so to speak, that He must reprimand us

---

[169] Pirke Avot 1:3

Penine Ḥaim

and issue judgements for those mistakes. Hashem does not want to see his children punished and in any form of pain. In this vein, the prophet Yishayahu[170] laments: "Why are you being beaten, and still add further rebellion?" The Jews were getting beaten and punished for their sins, yet they were adding a second, further rebellion: when we are afflicted because of our sins, it pains Hashem that He must discipline us. When a child misbehaves and must be disciplined, he causes extra pain to his father, not only by the act of misbehaving, but also by forcing his father to discipline him.

With this idea we can understand the suggestion of the Gemara that Moshe was seeking to receive reward for entering the land of Israel. Moshe's desire for reward was not selfish. Moshe wanted to fulfill the mitzvot of the land and receive reward for them, not for personal gain, but to give Hashem the "pleasure" of being able to reward His children. When Hashem rewards us, it gives Him happiness to be able to shower us with those blessings.

Likewise, our service to Hashem should be driven by love and respect for our Father in Heaven. When we do good, we not only benefit ourselves, we also bring joy to Hashem. May we always make positive choices and continue to bring Hashem "pleasure," ultimately receiving health and prosperity ourselves. Amen.

---

[170] Yishayahu 1:5

פרשת עקב

Parashat Ekev

The Value of All Mitzvot

וְהָיָה עֵקֶב תִּשְׁמְעוּן אֵת הַמִּשְׁפָּטִים הָאֵלֶּה וּשְׁמַרְתֶּם וַעֲשִׂיתֶם אֹתָם וְשָׁמַר ה'
אֱ-לֹהֶיךָ לְךָ אֶת הַבְּרִית וְאֶת הַחֶסֶד אֲשֶׁר נִשְׁבַּע לַאֲבֹתֶיךָ:

"And it will be if you do obey these laws and observe them carefully, Hashem your God will maintain faithfully for you the covenant He made on oath with your fathers."[171]

Our Parasha opens with a simple promise: keep Hashem's mitzvot, and blessings will follow. "It will be when - *Ekev* - you will obey these laws," Hashem will maintain his promise and bless us. The verse opens, however, with the unusual Hebrew word *Ekev*, which normally means "heel." What does the word *Ekev* signify? Rashi[172] quotes the Midrash which explains that the word "*Ekev*" describes the type of mitzvot which the blessing is referring to. The Torah is referring to those mitzvot w people "trample with their

---

[171] Devarim 7:12
[172] Rashi Devarim 7:12

heel" by deeming them minor or unimportant. Unfortunately, there are some mitzvot that people attribute more value to in comparison to other mitzvot, for whatever reason. Moshe Rabbenu says that who keep those mitzvot which are being neglected by others will merit to all the blessings in the Torah.

The lesson of the Midrash is that we should never decide based on personal judgement which mitzvot are more important than others. There are often great misconceptions that are unfortunately prevalent when it comes to weighing the mitzvot. For example, for many people who did not learn, keeping Yom Kippur once a year is much more important than keeping Shabbat on a weekly basis. There are many who will be extremely meticulous when it comes to fasting and keeping all the laws of the day of Yom Kippur but will then be lax when it comes to observing the day of Shabbat and its laws. This perspective is completely incorrect: one who learns the laws of Shabbat and laws of Yom Kippur will see that neglecting the observance of Shabbat requires a greater atonement than neglecting the observance of Yom Kippur. Although we are required to safeguard both to the fullest degree, the laws of atonement for sins show that violating Shabbat may be more severe than violating Yom Kippur. Therefore, instead than judging whether one mitzvah is more or less important than the other, we should observe all the laws of the Torah equally and to their fullest.

When considering the mitzvot of the Torah, an important principle must be remembered: we should not judge the worth of the mitzvot based on their content, but rather on Who gave us the commandments: Hashem Himself. All the mitzvot are directives from our Father in Heaven to connect us to Him; therefore, every single mitzvah is important. As Pirke Avot[173] teaches, "be

---

[173] Pirke Avot 2:1

meticulous when observing both the 'lighter' and 'heavier' mitzvot since you never know their real reward." Therefore, we should not prioritize one mitzvah over another mitzvah. Each mitzvah deserves equal dedication and equal excitement. May we merit to fulfill all Hashem's commandments with joy and receive the abundance of blessings promised in the Torah, Amen.

פרשת ראה

Parashat Re'eh

More Than Food: The Spiritual Significance of Kashrut

לֹא תֹאכַל כָּל תּוֹעֵבָה : זֹאת הַבְּהֵמָה אֲשֶׁר תֹּאכֵלוּ

"You shall not eat any abomination. These are the animals that you may eat..."[174]

The story is told of a young rabbi who was appointed as the spiritual leader of a new community. After his first few months, he noticed that he was unsuccessful in inspiring his community with his heartfelt sermons and classes. He went to his personal rabbi to seek advice. The elder rabbi told him, "Give sermons to your congregation about eating only kosher and refraining from non-kosher, this is the most important topic." The next few Shabbats, the young rabbi preached about the importance of Kashrut, and requested that community members should keep strict kosher standards and eat only kosher for a full month.

---

[174] Devarim 14:3-4

By the end of the month, the rabbi noticed his sermons were beginning to have more impact on his congregants. Amazed by the results, the younger rabbi went back to his rabbi for an explanation. His rabbi responded, "The food one eats has a great impact on one's soul. The more one eats non-kosher, the more spiritual blockages are made on his heart which make it more difficult to listen to Divre Torah. This is the reason I instructed you to urge your congregants to modify their diets. In some ways, you are what you eat, even spiritually."

In our Parasha, the Torah delineates the laws regarding keeping kosher. In Parashat Shemini, when describing the effects of non-kosher food on an individual, the Torah[175] states "*Venitmetem Bam*"- "you shall be contaminated through them." The Gemara[176] expounds this verse and says, "do not read the verse as saying you will become <u>contaminated</u> by eating non-kosher, rather read the verse as saying you will become <u>obstructed</u> by eating non-kosher." Although any sin can potentially obstruct the mind and heart from hearing the wisdom of the Torah, eating non-kosher in particular causes such spiritual blockages to form on a person's heart and makes it difficult for one to listen to Divre Torah.

Elsewhere, the Gemara[177] teaches that there is special Divine protection for truly righteous individuals to never stumble and eat non-kosher food. When a person is truly righteous, Hashem protects him or her from ingesting non-kosher food even by accident. We must take utmost precaution to only eat foods with proper kosher supervision. The importance of keeping Kashrut applies in all places, whether we are at home, at work, or on vacation. With

---

[175] Vayikra 11:43
[176] Yoma 39a
[177] Gittin 7a as explained by Tosafot ad. loc. D"H Hashta, and many other places.

Hashem's help, the merit of keeping the laws of Kashrut will open our hearts and our souls to appreciate and understand the holy words of the Torah for all the days of our lives.

פרשת שפטים

Parashat Shofetim

Upholding Honesty in Every Step

צֶדֶק צֶדֶק תִּרְדֹּף לְמַעַן תִּחְיֶה וְיָרַשְׁתָּ אֶת הָאָרֶץ אֲשֶׁר ה' אֱ-לֹהֶיךָ נֹתֵן לָךְ :

"Justice, justice you shall pursue, that you may thrive and occupy the land that Hashem your God is giving you."[178]

Honesty is a cornerstone of Judaism. Especially in legal matters, truth and justice must be the end goal. The Torah emphasizes the need to seek justice by stating: "Justice, Justice you shall pursue." We know well that the Torah does not repeat words unnecessarily. Why does the Torah use the double language of "Justice, Justice"? The Torah is stressing a deep principle to us: justice is not only about the end goal, but also about the entire journey. The means of attaining an honest goal must be honest and just as well. For example, deceiving others in business with the end goal of donating more money to charity is not acceptable. Although the end goal of giving charity may be one of the most noble pursuits, the ends do

---

[178] Devarim 16:20

not justify the means. Similarly, when teaching Torah, a teacher may not alter or fabricate any stories or principles in Judaism to sway people to keep more mitzvot. Teachers must be real and honest in their presentation of Torah. The path to achieve our goals must be as pure as our goals themselves.

The Gemara[179] beautifully quotes the verse in Sefer Shemuel[180] that as a judge, David Hamelech would engage in doing "justice <u>and</u> charity." Justice means delivering an honest ruling irrespective of which litigant is wealthy or poor. Charity means favoring the poor who are more in need than the wealthy. These two concepts appear to be contradictory – how did David Hamelech accomplish both at the same time? The Gemara explains that David Hamelech would always seek the truth. This meant that when evidence showed that a poor person was guilty in a case against a rich person, David Hamelech would rule with justice, in favor of the rich, even when the poor could not afford it. However, after rendering justice, David Hamelech would then assist the poor from his own funds as charity to support the poor litigant. David Hamelech did not sacrifice the truth for the sake of charity. He fulfilled both ideals in their own independent way.

In this context, Rav Ben-Haim mentioned an anecdote about his close friend Rav Asher Abittan z"l. Rabbi Abittan would recount that when he went to visit his native homeland of Morocco, he went to meet with one of the rabbis of the community there. When he got there, there was a Jew and an Arab who came to the rabbi for civil litigation. The rabbi reviewed the case and pressured the Jew by reminding him of the dangers of lying and swearing falsely in court. After the rabbi's efforts, the rabbi convinced the Jew to resolve the

---

[179] Sanhedrin 6b
[180] Shemuel 2 8:15

conflict honestly and pay the Arab what he owed. Seeing this incident, Rabbi Abittan approached the Arab and asked, "why did you come to the rabbi to be judged instead of going to the Mahkameh (i.e. sharia court)? The Arab replied, "I know that the judges of the local Mahkameh [Sharia court] accept bribes, and I know that the Jewish litigant is a corrupt man who would certainly bribe them. However, I also know that the rabbi does not accept bribes and would only judge honesty. Therefore, I sought the rabbi to adjudicate our case." This story shows how much the rabbi was recognized for his honesty.

We must uphold this legacy of honesty. Both the ends and the means of our pursuits must be fully honest and pure. We must model truth and justice and inspire the world through our integrity.

פרשת כי תצא

Parashat Ki Tetze

Married to Trouble: The Consequences of Conversion

וְרָאִיתָ בַּשִּׁבְיָה אֵשֶׁת יְפַת תֹּאַר וְחָשַׁקְתָּ בָה וְלָקַחְתָּ לְךָ לְאִשָּׁה:

"And you see among the captives a beautiful woman and you desire her, you may take [her] for yourself as a wife."[181]

The Gemara[182] records a troubling story: David Hamelech, perhaps our greatest king, requested to worship idols! One of his close friends, Ḥushai the Archite, asked him, "How can a king as great and righteous as you request to transgress one of the most severe sins of the Torah?" David Hamelech replied, "My son Avshalom is pursuing me to kill me. If I do not worship idols, people will come to question how Hashem could make it that a righteous king would be attacked by his own son. It would be better that I worship idols, and people will say that I deserved to have my son kill me because

---

[181] Devarim 21:11
[182] Sanhedrin 107a

I am a wicked person who worships idols, rather than to let Hashem's name be desecrated in public. There is one thing worse than the sin of worshipping idols, and that would be for Hashem's name to be desecrated in public." Ḥushai replied, "David, the reason why you have a son who wants to kill you is for one reason only: because you married an *Eshet Yefat To'ar*, a captive woman, the daughter of the non-Jewish King of Geshur, and you converted her for marriage. Your rebellious son was a result of this relationship with the princess of Geshur." David Hamelech protested: "But the Torah (in the beginning of our Parasha) permits a man to marry such a woman who he finds captive in war! I did not transgress any prohibition in the Torah." "That is true," Ḥushai replied, "but you did not pay attention to the Torah passage which follows. The passage right after the passage regarding a captive woman teaches, "If a man has a wayward and rebellious son..." The juxtaposition of these two passages teaches that even though the Torah does not prohibit a man to convert a non-Jewish captive of war and marry her, the product of this union will still be a rebellious and wayward son. David Hamelech indeed did this - he married the daughter of the King of Geshur that he saw in battle. His son Avshalom, who was the product of this relationship, eventually grew up to rebel against his own father. Therefore, people would not question Hashem's justice on the matter of Avshalom's rebellion. David Hamelech deserved what he received for marrying a captive woman. This story emphasizes the importance of careful consideration before conversion and marriage. Sincere converts who are inspired by genuine faith are certainly welcome. Some of the most righteous women in our history, such as Rut (the great-grandmother of David Hamelech) and Raḥav (who eventually married Yehoshua) were converts. They were exemplary righteous women who were drawn to Judaism by their love of Hashem, even with nothing to gain from becoming Jewish. However, when a convert is motivated by external factors, such as marriage, unintended consequences can arise. The Mashadi Jewish community, for example, exemplifies this caution. The community refuses any converts for marriage, male or female, regardless of any consideration, to protect against the risk of insincere conversions and their consequences. This Torah here highlights the importance of careful consideration before marriage. External motivations should not guide our spouse selection. Instead, we should seek compatible values which will enable building a family that is grounded on the values and principles of the Torah.

פרשת כי תבוא

Parashat Ki Tavo

The Key to Happiness

וְשָׂמַחְתָּ בְכָל הַטּוֹב אֲשֶׁר נָתַן לְךָ ה' אֱ-לֹהֶיךָ וּלְבֵיתֶךָ אַתָּה וְהַלֵּוִי וְהַגֵּר אֲשֶׁר
בְּקִרְבֶּךָ:

"Then, you shall rejoice with all the good that Hashem, your God has granted you and your household, you, the Levi, and the stranger who is among you."[183]

This week's Parasha introduces the unique mitzvah of Bikkurim. In the times when we had a Bet Hamikdash, when one planted fruit in Israel, he would bring the first fruits that were grown each year to the Bet Hamikdash and donate them as an expression of thanks to Hashem.

The Torah emphasizes that this mitzvah must be fulfilled with joy and gratefulness. "Then, you shall rejoice with all the good that Hashem, your God, has granted you." How does this act of offering

---

[183] Devarim 26:11

just a few fruits in the Bet Hamikdash evoke such happiness? What change can it bring to an individual?

The Torah here teaches us a crucial principle: true happiness does not come from attaining material possessions. Rather, it stems from the attitude towards what we already have. Pirke Avot[184] teaches: "Who is happy? One who is content with his lot." Genuine happiness does not necessarily come from owning large homes, or by driving a luxury car, or by wearing designer clothes. Genuine happiness comes from a person finding contentment with what he already has and expressing gratitude for the blessings he receives from Hashem. Happiness is a state of mind that every person can achieve by being grateful, even for the smallest things.

The mitzvah of Bikkurim exemplifies this message. Bikkurim represents the ability to see the first fruits of one's labor and to express gratitude even upon accomplishing a small milestone after much hard work. By dedicating these first fruits, we recognize that all our success ultimately stems from Hashem. This generates true joy – happiness that is found in being grateful for what we have, not being resentful for what we lack. Many people live in large houses and drive expensive cars, yet experience inner turmoil due to jealousy and anxiety over what they lack. On the other hand, there are many who live simply and sleep peacefully at night being satisfied and content. Having a healthy perspective and being content is life's greatest blessing.

In the end of the day, happiness in life is based on our perspective, not our possessions. If we constantly focus on what we lack, we will always be unhappy no matter how much we have. The mitzvah of Bikkurim teaches us that we can choose happiness by cultivating

---

[184] Pirke Avot 4:1

gratitude for even the smallest blessings. This will allow us to live a truly satisfied and content life for many years to come, Amen.

פרשת נצבים

Parashat Nitzavim

The Torah is Within Reach

כִּי הַמִּצְוָה הַזֹּאת אֲשֶׁר אָנֹכִי מְצַוְּךָ הַיּוֹם לֹא נִפְלֵאת הִוא מִמְּךָ וְלֹא רְחֹקָה הִוא:
לֹא בַשָּׁמַיִם הִוא לֵאמֹר מִי יַעֲלֶה לָּנוּ הַשָּׁמַיְמָה וְיִקָּחֶהָ לָּנוּ וְיַשְׁמִעֵנוּ אֹתָהּ וְנַעֲשֶׂנָּה:

"Surely, this Instruction which I am instructing you this day is not too baffling for you, nor is it beyond reach. It is not in the heavens that you should say, "Who among us can go up to the heavens and get it for us and impart it to us, so that we may observe it?"[185]

This week's Parasha features a famous verse in which Moshe emphasizes the accessibility of following the Torah and its commandments. Moshe assures everyone that observing the Torah is within reach for every person. Moshe uses a unique comparison: "It is not in the heavens, that you should say, "Who among us can go up to the heavens and get it for us." What point is Moshe trying to convey by stating that the Torah is "not in the heavens?"

---

[185] Devarim 30:11-12

Rashi[186] comments that Moshe was stating: "You do not need to chase the Torah in heavens, since it is not there. But if it was in the heavens, you would have had to develop a way to travel there to study and practice it." From this comment we can see that our rabbis had already understood many years ago that it is possible for mankind to travel to space!

There is a critical principle that we learn from this passage: Hashem never asks of us to do the impossible. The Torah and its commandments are not only beneficial for us, but they are also achievable for everyone as well. While the Torah's vast breadth and intricate details might seem daunting, we must remember that Hashem would not expect of us to live an impossible way of life. The mitzvot are attainable and incredibly rewarding when we consistently study and practice them.

To further illustrate this point, the Maggid Midovna[187] quotes the pasuk from the prophet Yishayahu[188] that says: "You have not worshipped Me, Yaakov, that you should be weary of Me, Israel." What is the meaning of this verse?

The Maggid explains with a parable: A man checks into a hotel with a small duffle bag. The bellhop, wanting a large tip, offers to take the guest's bag for him. As the bellhop brings the bag up to the room, he pretends the bag is heavy and gets to the room short of breath, wiping sweat off his face. The guest pays no attention and gives the bell boy a small tip. The bell boy began to complain that he worked so hard to bring the back up and he deserves a larger tip. The guest responded: "My duffle bag is small and light. If you were truly sweating so hard to bring it up, you must have been carrying

---

[186] Rashi Devarim 30:12
[187] Mishle Yaakov Parashat Nitzavim Mashal #413
[188] Yishayahu 43:22

someone else's duffle bag!" Similarly, Hashem says: "If you are weary from my mitzvot, then you have not been following My Torah. You must be worshipping something else." This is the meaning of the verse in Yishayahu. The Torah is pleasant and within reach to every person who wants to cling on to its timeless principles and values. Let us never forget the sweetness and accessibility of the Torah in all aspects of our lives. When we truly commit to dedicating ourselves to the Torah, we will see the beauty in observing every mitzvah, Amen.

פרשת וילך

Parashat Vayelech

Direct Access: The Mitzvah of Writing a Sefer Torah

וְעַתָּה כִּתְבוּ לָכֶם אֶת הַשִּׁירָה הַזֹּאת וְלַמְּדָהּ אֶת בְּנֵי יִשְׂרָאֵל שִׂימָה בְּפִיהֶם

"And now, write down this song and teach it to the people of Israel, place it in their mouths."[189]

In our Parasha, Moshe instructs the Jewish people to write down "this song" and teach it to the Jewish people. At the simple level, Rashi[190] and Ramban[191] both assert that the "song" in this verse refers to the song of Haazinu, which comes right after this Parasha. According to them, Moshe was instructed to write down the song and teach it well to the Jews, because the song of Haazinu teaches the Jewish nation about their history and future in a condensed format. The Gemara,[192] however, expounds that the song refers to

---

[189] Devarim 31:19
[190] Rashi Devarim 31:9
[191] Ramban 31:19
[192] Sanhedrin 21b

the entire Torah. This verse, in fact, is the source of the mitzvah for every Jew to write a Sefer Torah for himself. Even if a person inherited a Sefer Torah from his parents or grandparents, it is a mitzvah for every Jew to write his own Sefer Torah for himself.

Why is writing a Sefer Torah so important? The answer is because Hashem prioritizes literacy for everyone. There are many cultures in which only a religious leader can speak and know the language of their canon. In such cultures, the common person is expected to be illiterate, and to rely completely on the religious leader to understand the doctrines of their faith. For the Jewish nation, however, illiteracy is unacceptable. Hashem desires for every person to know how to read and write the holy language. This way, every person can directly access the text of the Torah itself without relying on intermediaries. Direct access to the Torah eliminates any hierarchy in terms of understanding the sacred text.

Rabbenu Asher, also known as the Rosh,[193] very famously suggested that nowadays one can fulfill the mitzvah of writing a Sefer Torah by buying other religious books (Sefarim) as opposed to writing or purchasing an actual Sefer Torah scroll. Since it is more common nowadays to study from books, and a Sefer Torah normally remains inside the Hechal at the synagogue most of the time, the primary mitzvah nowadays is to purchase religious books for oneself. While it is certainly praiseworthy to fulfill this opinion by purchasing Sefarim to learn and read at home, the practical halacha is that we still must write or purchase an actual Sefer Torah scroll for ourselves to fulfill this mitzvah.[194] May we all merit to fulfill the mitzvah of writing our own Sefer Torah and have the merit to read and learn from it, Amen.

---

[193] Rosh Halachot Sefer Torah 3
[194] Shulḥan Aruch Yoreh Deah 270:1

פרשת האזינו

Parashat Haazinu

History as Our Witness: The Remarkable Journey of Our Nation

הַאֲזִינוּ הַשָּׁמַיִם וַאֲדַבֵּרָה וְתִשְׁמַע הָאָרֶץ אִמְרֵי פִי:

"Listen, O heavens, and I will speak! And let the earth hear the words of my mouth!"[195]

The question is often asked: as Jews, how can we be so confident that the Torah is Divine and from Hashem? One of the answers to this question can be found in Parashat Haazinu. At the beginning of this week's Parasha, Moshe Rabbenu charges the Heavens and the Earth as witnesses to his words.

In a powerful prophecy, Moshe Rabbenu predicts the future exile of the Jewish people and suffering for their sins. Moshe Rabbenu also assures that Hashem will never abandon us and will bring us back to Israel. If there was any similar story in the history of any other nation, perhaps we could question how meaningful the prophecy of

---

[195] Devarim 32:1

Haazinu is. But no other nation's history features such a unique experience: a nation that was exiled from their land for close to 2000 years followed by a return to rebuild their homeland. The Torah, written over three thousand years ago, accurately recorded these events. Moshe Rabbenu's predictions defied any human reasoning or logic. The Jewish people were scattered across the four corners of the earth for so many years. We managed to preserve our Jewish identity in every country we lived in, through persecution and suffering, yet we were not wiped out and we came back to rebuild our homeland. The fact that we fulfilled this prophecy in our history points to the Divine origin of the Torah.

In Parashat Ki Tavo, Moshe Rabbenu says that if the Jewish does not follow the Torah, we will be persecuted by a brazen nation.[196] What does Moshe mean by a brazen nation? Our rabbis describe that brazenness is one of the character traits of an illegitimate child (*mamzer*).[197] Indeed, we find that Adolf Hilter, may his name be erased, the man responsible for the unimaginable horror of the Holocaust was born from an illegitimate child. Hilter's father, Alois Hitler, was an illegitimate child born out of wedlock, and had an unknown biological father. The Torah indicated that someone like this would be born, a man who had no shame committing genocide and being responsible for the mass murder of children, the elderly, and the most vulnerable people of society.

In our Parasha, Hashem says, "I will finish my arrows against the Jews." The Gemara[198] explains that Hashem is, so to speak, implying that His arrows will finish, yet the Jewish nation will not be finished. In other words, despite the hardships and persecution

---

[196] Devarim 28:50
[197] Kalla Rabbati 2:1
[198] Sota 9a

we faced throughout our history, the Jewish nation will persevere and survive.

After so many years, the Jewish nation has come together from all over the globe to rebuild our land, the land of Israel. Israel's growth and strength is remarkable. When the state was first founded, Rav Ben-Haim reports that he remembers how there was a scarcity of food. Food was being rationed. To survive, people would eat the French mallow plant (known as khubeiza in Arabic). Nobody could have imagined how miraculously the land of Israel has come to flourish, and how remarkably strong the State of Israel has become, Baruch Hashem. The miracle of our history is the greatest testament to the truth of the Torah, strengthening our faith in Hashem and the holy words of the Torah.

פרשת וזאת הברכה

Parashat Vezot Haberacha

The Missing Blessing: Intermarriage and the Future of Judaism

וְזֹאת הַבְּרָכָה אֲשֶׁר בֵּרַךְ מֹשֶׁה אִישׁ הָאֱ-לֹהִים אֶת בְּנֵי יִשְׂרָאֵל לִפְנֵי מוֹתוֹ :

"And this is the blessing with which Moshe, the man of God, blessed the children of Israel before his death."[199]

The majority of our Parasha features Moshe Rabbenu's very last blessings to each Jewish tribe before his death. Moshe begins by blessing the tribe of Reuven, then Yehuda, followed by Levi. One tribe is blessed after the other. Notably, one tribe is missing from the blessings: the tribe of Shimon. Where is Shimon? Why did Moshe exclude them from his final blessings?

Ramban[200] suggests that Shimon was left out because the tribe of Shimon was a smaller tribe than the other tribes. Earlier in Parashat Vayḥi, Yaakov Avinu had only blessed Shimon that he would be

---

[199] Devarim 33:1
[200] Ramban Devarim 33:6

spread out amongst the other tribes. Now that Shimon was spread out amongst the other tribes, a blessing was unnecessary. Ibn Ezra[201] adds that Moshe Rabbenu purposely excluded Shimon and didn't give him a blessing. He excluded Shimon for one very serious reason: intermarriage. Earlier in Torah, the leader of Shimon, Zimri, married the princess of Mo'ab. Most of the tribe of Shimon followed suit and married outside the faith and into the non-Jewish tribes of Mo'ab. This resulted in a plague that significantly damaged the Jewish nation.

Intermarriage threatens the future of Judaism by severing the future generations' connection to our faith. Therefore, Moshe Rabbenu treated the sin of intermarriage as exceptionally severe. Previously in the Torah, Moshe was able to forgive the other sins of the Jews. As much as the other tribes also sinned in the Torah, those tribes remained part of the Jewish nation. Intermarriage, however, opened the door to complete disconnect and threatened the existence of the Jewish people. Moshe therefore could not bring himself to bless the tribe of Shimon.

This episode highlights the severity of intermarriage. Rambam[202] writes that the sin of marrying a non-Jew should not be taken lightly - when a Jewish man marries a non-Jewish woman, the Torah says that one's children are no longer considered his own! They have been severed from the Jewish nation and are no longer considered the children of their father, even if they subsequently convert to Judaism. The sin of intermarriage is the single greatest threat to the continuity of the Jewish people. We must work to protect ourselves and our families from intermarriage, and that way we can ensure the

---

[201] Ibn Ezra Devarim 33:6
[202] Hilchot Issure Biah 12:7

perpetuation of our Torah and Jewish values for generations to come.

JEWISH
HOLIDAYS

Penine Ḥaim

ראש השנה

Rosh Hashana

The Shofar's Call: Waking Up and Taking Action

Rav Ben-Haim recalls one of the rabbis of Yerushalayim who once spoke many years ago on Rosh Hashana. The rabbi noted that David Hamelech was an incredibly mighty warrior. In the book of Shemuel,[203] he tells Shaul Hamelech, "Your servant has killed lions and bears!" In other words, David Hamelech was mightier than even lions and bears and was capable of killing them on his own. At the same time, we find that in the book of Tehillim,[204] David Hamelech writes about Hashem, "My skin shudders from fear of You, and I dread Your judgements." Despite his immense strength and not being afraid of even a lion or a bear, David Hamelech expressed awe and fear before Hashem's judgements. Therefore, when we stand to be judged before Hashem on the day of Rosh Hashana, we must approach the days with a sense of awe and trepidation. Although the Vilna Gaon[205] notes that the day of Rosh Hashana is a joyous

---

[203] Shemuel 1 17:36
[204] Tehillim 119:120
[205] Maase Rav #207

holiday where we crown Hashem as our King, we must also approach the day with seriousness and a sense of awe.

Rambam[206] famously writes that the sound of the shofar on Rosh Hashana contains a deep allusion. The sounds of the shofar call out to us to wake up from our spiritual slumber, to reflect on our actions, and to repent before Hashem. During the year, many people get lost in worldly pursuits and devote their energies to vanity and emptiness, which will not benefit or save them. On Rosh Hashana, we must focus on how we can improve ourselves and make meaningful changes with the guidance of the Torah as our light. On Rosh Hashana, every person should see himself as equally balanced between good and bad, and the world as equally balanced between good and bad. Every sin tips the scale of the entire world to the side towards negativity. On the other hand, every mitzvah tips the scale of the entire world to the side of merit and life.

The Maggid Midovna tells a beautiful parable that relates to Rosh Hashana. A doctor once gave a prescription to a man who was sick with a terrible illness. When the man came home, he told his wife that he was diagnosed with a life-threatening illness, and the doctor gave him a paper with a prescription to get better. The man then asked his wife for tea. When his wife brought the tea, he took the paper with the prescription, dissolved it into the tea and drank it. "You fool!", his wife said to him. "The paper itself is not your healing! Following the doctor's instructions that were written on the paper is your healing! Drinking a piece of paper will not help you at all."

The same often happens to us. People often assume that going through the motions and kissing the Torah scroll on Rosh Hashana is our healing. Unfortunately, this is not true. Kissing a parchment

---

[206] Hilchot Teshuva 3:4

of Torah without sincerity or commitment does not provide any benefit. It is following the true teachings of Torah and its sacred commandments that brings us healing, spiritual growth and fulfillment. May we all be blessed with a meaningful Rosh Hashana, leading to complete Teshuva and a year filled with blessings.

יום כיפור

Yom Kippur

Beyond Forgiveness: The Importance of Teshuva on Yom Kippur

The Gemara[207] presents different opinions about whether the day of Yom Kippur inherently atones for sins, regardless of the Jews actually doing Teshuva. Rabbi Yehuda Hanasi maintained that the day of Yom Kippur provides atonement for all sins, regardless of whether a person does Teshuva or does not. On the other hand, the majority of the sages disagreed and said that a person must repent to achieve atonement on Yom Kippur. Rambam[208] rules in accordance with the majority, emphasizing that repentance is necessary step to achieve atonement on Yom Kippur.

The above passage raises a question. According to Rabbi Yehuda Hanasi, if the very day of Yom Kippur atones for all the sins of the Jewish people regardless of whether we do Teshuva or not, how could the Bet Hamikdash be destroyed on account of our sins? If all our sins were erased with every Yom Kippur that passed, there

---

[207] Yoma 85b
[208] Hilchot Teshuva 1:3

should not have been any sins remaining that the Bet Hamikdash should be destroyed on their account.

This contradiction can be explained based on a parable about a man named Shimon. Shimon, a reckless driver, consistently broke traffic laws. One day, Shimon ran a red light while speeding, and did not notice that a truck that was coming from the other direction. The truck unfortunately slammed into his car and left Shimon with permanent injuries from head to toe due to the accident. Shimon suffered broken bones, severe bruising, and major blood loss. After several months in the hospital with intense treatments and recovery, Shimon, now bound to a wheelchair, was summoned to court to answer for the ticket for the red-light violation. When the judge saw Shimon's physical state and suffering, he showed mercy and declared: "not guilty!" However, even though Shimon was absolved of the fine for running the red light, the accident's physical consequences remained. Even though the judge declared that Shimon was "not guilty," this ruling did not help heal Shimon's injuries from the accident.

This parable describes us and our situation when it comes to our sins on Yom Kippur. Hashem is certainly a merciful and forgiving King, and we are confident that during this time of year, He will forgive our sins. However, at the end of the day, a sin itself carries consequences. Our sins themselves tarnish our souls and can cause harm, regardless of whether Hashem holds us accountable or not. Even if Hashem forgives us on Yom Kippur and forgives the "ticket," the damage from a sin remains until we do a complete Teshuva. Only a complete teshuva process, with sincere introspection, regret, and rectification, can repair the damage caused by sin. According to the opinion of Rabbi Yehuda Hanasi, this is how we can explain that the Bet Hamikdash was destroyed. Even though Hashem is merciful and forgave the sins of the Jewish people every year, their sins continued to have harmful effects because they did not do Teshuva.

During this time of year, Hashem is exceptionally close to us and available to forgive our sins. However, only a complete Teshuva process can cure the inherent damage brought about by our sins. Let us take advantage of this special opportunity for repentance and forgiveness and return to Hashem and to the ways of His Torah with all of our hearts and souls.

סוכות

Sukkot

Sharing Our Joy with All of Am Yisrael

כְּשֵׁם שֶׁמִּצְוָה לְכַבֵּד שַׁבָּת וּלְעַנְּגָהּ, כָּךְ כָּל יָמִים טוֹבִים... חַיָּב אָדָם לִהְיוֹת בָּהֶן שָׂמֵחַ וְטוֹב לֵב, הוּא וּבָנָיו וְאִשְׁתּוֹ וּבְנֵי בֵּיתוֹ וְכָל הַנִּלְוִים עָלָיו, שֶׁנֶּאֱמַר "וְשָׂמַחְתָּ בְּחַגֶּךָ . . ." (דברים טז,יד)... וּכְשֶׁהוּא אוֹכֵל וְשׁוֹתֶה, חַיָּב לְהַאֲכִיל לַגֵּר לַיָּתוֹם וְלָאַלְמָנָה עִם שְׁאָר הָעֲנִיִּים הָאֻמְלָלִים. אֲבָל מִי שֶׁנּוֹעֵל דַּלְתוֹת חֲצֵרוֹ וְאוֹכֵל וְשׁוֹתֶה הוּא וּבָנָיו וְאִשְׁתּוֹ, וְאֵינוּ מַאֲכִיל וּמַשְׁקֶה לָעֲנִיִּים וּלְמָרֵי נֶפֶשׁ אֵין זוֹ שִׂמְחַת מִצְוָה, אֶלָּא שִׂמְחַת כְּרֵסוֹ.

"Just as it is a mitzvah to celebrate and be happy on Shabbat, so too it is a mitzvah to celebrate and be happy on Yom Tov, along with one's family and those who depend on him, as the pasuk says, "You shall rejoice on your holiday..." When one feasts with his family, he is required to include the converts, orphans, widows, and others who suffer from poverty. He who closes himself off from people in need and feeds only his family while neglecting the poor and destitute - his joy on the holiday is not a mitzvah but a selfish act, aimed only at his own gut."[209]

---

[209] Rambam, Laws of Yom Tov 6:16-18

In the above passage, Rambam emphasizes the obligation to provide financial support to the poor during the holiday season. If one neglects to provide support to the poor during the holidays, his holiday celebration is not a mitzvah at all, it is only a selfish act aimed only at his own gut. Why does Rambam say that one is not considered to be performing a mitzvah if one does not give support to the poor on the holidays? The following parable adapted from the Maggid Midovna illustrates this principle eloquently.

A wealthy man was once preparing for the wedding celebration of his youngest son. The joy was limitless, and the man spared no expense to make the wedding the most magnificent and memorable celebration possible. The man also had two older sons living abroad with their families. One son was wealthy, while the other struggled financially. When news of the engagement went public, he called his wealthy son and gave him the following instructions: "Please prepare your family and your brother's family to come for the upcoming wedding. Spare no expense; every dollar that you spend towards the wedding in my honor will be fully reimbursed."

The son was thrilled to hear the good news! He now had the opportunity to spend as freely as he wanted, with guaranteed reimbursement! He, his wife, and his children spent the next week purchasing designer clothing, jewelry, first class tickets, and other extravagant luxuries. As an afterthought, the wealthy son purchased basic plane tickets for his poor brother and his family as well.

When the two brothers arrived at the airport on the morning of the wedding, the father was mortified. The successful son and his family showed up in their new clothes, looking like royalty, but the poor son and his family were still wearing their worn-out second-hand clothing. The father quickly made arrangements to get proper attire for his poor son and his family for the wedding later that night.

The party turned out to be a magnificent event. It carried on until the early hours of the morning in splendor and extravagance. The next morning, before returning home, the successful son approached his father to collect the promised reimbursement of his expenditures. But all he got was a pat on the back and a farewell.

"Father," he protested, "don't you remember our agreement? I spend thousands of dollars, and you promised to repay me!"

"That is not what I promised," the father told him. "My instructions were clear: every dollar that you spend towards the wedding <u>in my honor</u> will be fully reimbursed. If your expenses were genuinely spent <u>in my honor</u>, you would have cared for your poor brother, so he would make a grand appearance at my party just as you did. Instead, you used it as an excuse to spruce up your own wardrobe and personally indulge yourself. Your motives were selfish, and I will not contribute to them."

The message behind this story is strikingly clear. When Yom Tov comes around, we often spend happily on food, new clothing, and other pleasures to make the holiday as enjoyable as we can. In fact, the Gemara tells us that there are three expenses that Hashem fully reimburses us for each year: what we spend towards Shabbat, Yom Tov and Jewish education.[210] However, if we are truly spending for the honor of the holiday, we must remember to provide those in need with the ability to celebrate the holiday properly as well. Those who neglect the poor and destitute expose that their holiday expenses are nothing more than a means to serve their selfish indulgences under the mask of worshipping Hashem, just like the selfish son who tried to expand his wardrobe at his father's expense. On the other hand,

---

[210] Betza 16a

when we provide support to those in need to celebrate the holiday properly with us, we demonstrate that our motives in celebrating the holiday are pure and directed towards Hashem and his commandments, and that our physical pleasures are truly reflections of the spiritual nature of the day.

May we merit to celebrate many holidays together, always remembering to include all of Am Yisrael in our joy.

חנוכה

Ḥanukkah

The Miracles We Remember

Over 2000 years ago, our rabbis established the holiday of Ḥanukkah to commemorate two miracles: The first miracle was the military success of the Maccabees, who recaptured the Bet Hamikdash from the hands of the powerful Seleucid Greeks. The second miracle was the miracle of the oil that lasted for eight days instead of one. It is striking to note that in the Al Hanisim prayer that is recited in the Amida during the eight days of Ḥanukkah, only the miracle of the military victory is mentioned. The miracle of the oil lasting eight days is not mentioned! Why does Al Hanisim omit any mention of the miracle of the oil?

The answer can be understood through the story of the Kuzari. Rabbi Yehuda Halevi, the author of the Kuzari, records a dialogue between the king of Khazars, a philosopher, a Muslim, and a Christian. The king asks each of these leaders for proof of Hashem's existence and to explain their belief system. After not being satisfied with any of their responses, the king finally turns to the Jew. Instead of offering the king abstract proofs of Hashem's existence, the Jew tells the story of how Hashem delivered the Jews from the bondage of Egypt and revealed himself to the Jews at Har Sinai, events which were all witnessed by millions of people.

The Jew explained that although he could have given the king numerous proofs for Hashem's existence, those proofs can also be disputed. But the shared historical experience, when Hashem saved the Jews from Egypt and revealed Himself to millions of Jews at Har Sinai, is a memory that is passed down from generation to generation. As part of our national memory, these events cannot be disputed.

Bearing this in mind, we can understand why the Al Hanisim prayer chooses to mention the miracle of the war and not the miracle of the oil. Even though the miracle of the small cruise of oil that lit for eight days was an awe-inspiring miracle to all those who saw it, at the end of the day, only a small few Kohanim who were serving in the Bet Hamikdash merited to see it. One who was not a Kohen serving in the Bet Hamikdash did not see the miracle directly. In a way, it was a hidden miracle.

On the other hand, the miracle of the military victory — the small band of heroic Jews who defeated the mighty Syrian-Greek army — was a public miracle for all to see. It was an undisputed miracle during which all people saw the hand of Hashem. Therefore, when the Rabbis established the Al Hanisim prayer, they preferred to mention the public miracle that all Jews witnessed rather than the private miracle that most did not witness firsthand.

On Ḥanukkah, let us remember all the miracles Hashem has done for us, public and private, and give Him our thanks for those miracles. We praise Hashem for delivering us from the hands of those who sought to destroy our identity and faith. Just as Hashem delivered the strong into the hands of weak and the many into the hands of the few, may He continue to bless and protect our nation for generations to come.

פורים

Purim

Two Holidays, Two Responses: Understanding Purim and Ḥanukkah

Purim stands out on the Jewish calendar for its joyous nature. In addition to the reading of Megillat Esther, the holiday celebrations emphasize our unity through festive meals and gift-giving, Mishloaḥ Manot and Matanot La'evyonim as part of the holiday.

When observing the celebration of Purim, one cannot help but realize that the emphasis is on physical and material celebration. On Purim, we must send food and gifts to others and have a festive meal to fulfill the mitzvot of the day. This is in stark contrast to the similar rabbinic holiday of Ḥanukkah, during which the mitzvot of the holiday appear to have the more spiritual focus we expect: lighting a menorah and reciting Hallel for eight days to praise Hashem for the miracles. Why does Purim seem to have such an opposite approach in comparison to Ḥanukkah?

The Levush[211] offers an explanation to the difference of approaches: Purim was the time in history in which the Jews faced genocide.

---

[211] Levush Halachot Ḥanukkah 670:2, quoted by Mishna Berura

Haman wanted to physically annihilate the Jews. Therefore, we celebrate the victory of Purim by engaging in physical acts such as feasting, sending gifts and drinking, and elevating them to the service of Hashem. Ḥanukkah, however, was different. The Seleucid Greeks did not necessarily want to exterminate us; rather, their goal was assimilation, not annihilation. They wanted us to eradicate our spiritual identity through Hellenism, by insisting that we relinquish our Jewish heritage to become like them. Therefore, we celebrate the victory over the Greeks by engaging in spiritual actions, emphasizing the spiritual core of the Jewish nation.

A fascinating observation can be made when comparing these two holidays. By Ḥanukkah, the response to the danger of the Jews was to engage in battle. The Maccabees united to wage war against their enemies and to revolt against the Greek efforts. The Books of 1 Maccabees[212] even describes how the Jews soldiers gave up their lives because they did not want to fight on Shabbat and desecrate the day. Matityahu Kohen Gadol, the leader of the Maccabees, ordered them to fight on Shabbat to ensure the safety of the Jewish nation and victory over the Greeks! On the other hand, during Purim, the Jews did not fight a war at all. Queen Esther called on the Jews to engage in fasting and spiritual reflection: "Go, assemble all the Jews who live in Shushan, and fast on my behalf; do not eat or drink for three days, night or day. I and my maidens will fast as well."[213] Esther wanted the Jews to work on themselves spiritually and pray Hashem for mercy. Only after the miracles of Purim unfolded and the Jews had the support of the King did they then go ahead and fight. The question can be asked: why the difference in response? Why on Ḥanukkah was the initial response to wage war, whereas by

---

[212] 1 Maccabees Chapter 2
[213] Esther 4:16

Purim the initial response was not warfare but spiritual introspection?

The Lubavitcher Rebbe offers the following insight: the jealousy of the gentiles reflects the strengths and weaknesses of the Jews. When the gentiles are not jealous of the Jews in a specific area, then that shows that we may be lacking in that area. During the days of Ḥanukkah, their target was our spirituality, indicating our spiritual strength and physical weakness. Being physically weak, the Maccabees called on the Jews to wage physical warfare to compensate for their weakness.

On Purim, however, our enemies envied our financial and socioeconomic success and wanted to physically annihilate us. This revealed that although the Jewish people were flourishing physically, they were lacking spiritually. Their participation in the feast of Aḥashverosh showed their lack of spirituality by wanting to be like the gentiles. Since the Jewish people were lacking spiritually, Esther called on the Jews to rectify this weakness. Therefore, she instructed them to fast and pray to Hashem for salvation. This explains the difference in responses when comparing Ḥanukkah and Purim. The envy of the gentiles highlighted the areas that required improvement at that point in Jewish history.

When looking at our current standing, there is much antisemitism from the outside world that concerns the financial success and stature of the Jews. Many Jewish communities are thriving and are experiencing prosperity, Baruch Hashem. However, this also may imply that we need to improve our spiritual endeavors. There is not much external envy, at this point, about the role of the Jews being a "light onto the nations." High rates of assimilation and lack of awareness of our Jewish identity shows that we may be lacking spiritually, and we must therefore work harder to strengthen our spirituality and Jewish identity. We must always remember that our status as a chosen nation by Hashem carries a strong responsibility with it. We should embrace our mission to share Torah values with the world us and be a global model as a light onto the nations.

פֶּסַח

Pesaḥ

The Wise and the Wicked

חָכָם מָה הוּא אוֹמֵר? מָה הָעֵדוֹת וְהַחֻקִּים וְהַמִּשְׁפָּטִים אֲשֶׁר צִוָּה ה' אֱ-לֹהֵינוּ
אֶתְכֶם. וְאַף אַתָּה אֱמוֹר לוֹ כְּהִלְכוֹת הַפֶּסַח: אֵין מַפְטִירִין אַחַר הַפֶּסַח אֲפִיקוֹמָן:
רָשָׁע מָה הוּא אוֹמֵר? מָה הָעֲבוֹדָה הַזֹּאת לָכֶם. לָכֶם – וְלֹא לוֹ. וּלְפִי שֶׁהוֹצִיא אֶת
עַצְמוֹ מִן הַכְּלָל כָּפַר בָּעִקָּר. וְאַף אַתָּה הַקְהֵה אֶת שִׁנָּיו וֶאֱמוֹר לוֹ: "בַּעֲבוּר זֶה
עָשָׂה ה' לִי בְּצֵאתִי מִמִּצְרָיִם." לִי וְלֹא לוֹ. אִלּוּ הָיָה שָׁם, לֹא הָיָה נִגְאָל:

*What does the wise son say? "What are these testimonies, statutes
and judgments that Hashem our God commanded you?'*[214] *And
accordingly you will say to him, as per the laws of the Pesaḥ
sacrifice, "We may not eat an afikoman [a dessert] after we are
finished eating the Pesaḥ sacrifice."*[215]

What does the evil son say? "What is this worship to you?"[216] *To
you and not to him. And since he excluded himself from the nation,
he denied a principle of the Jewish faith. Accordingly, you should
blunt his teeth and tell him, "For this reason, Hashem did [this] for*

---

[214] Devarim 6:20
[215] Mishna Pesaḥim 10:8
[216] Shemot 12:26

*me when I left Egypt."[217] For me and not for him. If he [the evil son]
had been there in Egypt, he would not have been saved.*

This well-known passage in the Haggadah describes to us the four
different types of sons present at the Pesaḥ Seder. A very famous
question is asked on this passage: Both the Wise and the Wicked son
appear to use similar language. The Wicked son says, "What is this
worship to <u>you</u> (לָכֶם)," while the Wise son says, "What are these
testimonies, statutes and judgments that Hashem our God
commanded <u>you</u> (אֶתְכֶם)? Both the Wise and the Wicked son appear
to exclude themselves by using the term "you," yet we only criticize
the Wicked son for using this term in his question. Why?

The Rabbis offer a beautiful answer. The wise son seeks clarity on
the laws and the practices that we are performing at the Seder. He
asks questions with a genuine desire to learn and understand all the
finest details. The Wicked son, on the other hand, does not aim to
learn. His main concern is "work" (עֲבוֹדָה), and he frames the Torah
as a burdensome task that he does not want to be part of. By saying
"What is this work you are doing?", he is mocking us for taking this
supposed burden on ourselves.

In the book of Mishle,[218] Shelomo Hamelech writes, "Its ways are
ways of pleasantness, and all its pathways are peace." When a task
is pleasant and enjoyable for us, we will happily do it and not feel
any burden, even if the task requires work. On the other hand, if a
task is unpleasant for us, even the most minimal effort will be a
burden. The Torah that Hashem gave us, when embraced with the
correct approach of love, is not a burden. The opposite - it enriches

---

[217] Shemot 13:8
[218] Mishle 3:17

and uplifts every part of our lives. This is why we criticize the Wicked son.

Let us carry this lesson with us into Pesaḥ. We should emulate the Wise son who asks questions with love and curiosity to learn and grow in his Torah knowledge. This is the purpose for which Hashem bestowed the Torah upon us – to ask questions with a passionate desire to learn more and become the next link in the chain of our beautiful Jewish heritage. Ḥag Sameaḥ!

יום העצמאות

Yom Haatzmaut

The Early Days of Israel

Rav Ben-Haim shared many personal memories from Israel in its earliest days. Rav Ben-Haim was a young boy, only seven years old at the time, living in Yerushalayim during the War of Independence in 1948. He remembers the day David Ben Gurion declared Israel's independence. It was on the 5th of Iyyar, on erev Shabbat. As soon as Ben Gurion made the announcement, the war began. The celebrations were short-lived. The non-stop sound of bullets being fired and shells striking the ground all around took their toll. Rav Ben-Haim could not forget the sight of the bodies of dead soldiers lying in the streets. There was almost no family living in Yerushalayim without a fallen soldier.

Israel's population at the time was around 800,000, while the combined population of the seven Arab countries attacking us was in the millions. Israel's military forces were severely outnumbered, both in number and supplies. There was a severe shortage of basic food and weapons. Rav Ben-Haim remembers how his uncle would travel to visit his family, having to use a dangerous road that was constantly under enemy fire, just to bring over a little bit of food - just enough to survive. The food shortage was so severe that people were forced to find wild plants to eat in the field. Everything of value was rationed, even such basics like water, flour, sugar, and oil. People had to wait in long lines just to bring home a bucket of water. Rav Ben-Haim has a vivid memory of how one time, a jug of oil accidentally spilled on the floor. The oil was so valuable to us, that everyone who was around rushed to soak up the oil from the floor with rags and squeeze it back into the jug. Nothing could go to waste. This was how difficult the situation became in Yerushalayim. The proclamation of Israel's independence was a risky decision. Many were against it, even within the People's Administration that was convened to vote on declaring independence. Baruch Hashem, the leaders of the time voted to declare independence. The fact that we were able to emerge from that war – seven Arab nations against one - was an undeniable miracle, especially so soon after the terrible destruction of the Holocaust. With Hashem's help, Israel emerged victorious.

Rav Ben-Haim also recalled the events of the Six Day War, only nineteen years later. This was a war during which every living Israeli witnessed open miracles with his own eyes. Once the threat from the Arab countries started to escalate and was taken more seriously, the masses were conscripted into the army, from the full spectrum of Israeli society. Huge fields were prepared as potential gravesites in case there would be mass casualties from the war. And then, the miracle began. Israel banded together, and for a short time in Israel's history, there were no divisions. The usually highly divided Israeli government banded together to form a National Unity government. Prime Minister Levi Eshkol gave up his position as Defense Minister to Moshe Dayan. Menachim Begin, a regular fixture in the

Israeli opposition, was allowed into the government, and this unity was the start of our path to victory. Rav Ben-Haim emphasized that Israel must always know and remember that our strength is in our unity, and our weakness only comes when we are divided. If we can care for one another and be willing to work together with the common goal of creating a stronger State of Israel, Israel's future will always be bright.

The contrast between Israel in those days and Israel today is beyond imagination. During those early days, nobody could imagine the extent to which Israel would be flourishing nowadays. Not only is there no food shortage, but also, Israel is exporting all types of products all over the world. Israel is an economic and military powerhouse in the region with a prosperous high-tech sector. With tremendous gratitude to Hashem, we can continue to say "Am Yisrael Ḥai."

שבועות

Shavuot

Accepting the Torah With Unity

בַּחֹדֶשׁ הַשְּׁלִישִׁי לְצֵאת בְּנֵי יִשְׂרָאֵל מֵאֶרֶץ מִצְרָיִם בַּיּוֹם הַזֶּה בָּאוּ מִדְבַּר סִינָי:
וַיִּסְעוּ מֵרְפִידִים וַיָּבֹאוּ מִדְבַּר סִינַי וַיַּחֲנוּ בַּמִּדְבָּר וַיִּחַן שָׁם יִשְׂרָאֵל נֶגֶד הָהָר:

In the third month, after the children of Israel had gone out of the land of Egypt, the same day they came into the wilderness of Sinai. Having journeyed from Rephidim, they entered the wilderness of Sinai and encamped in the wilderness. Israel encamped there in front of the mountain.[219]

Shavuot is one of the most important Jewish holidays, marking the day that the Ten Commandments were given to the Jewish people on Har Sinai.[220] When the Torah describes the Jewish people's arrival at the mountain, something unusual appears in the text. The Torah generally uses verbs in the plural form when referring to the Jewish nation as a whole. In this pasuk, however, when describing

---

[219] Shemot 19:1-2
[220] Shabbat 86b

their arrival at the mountain, the Torah uses the singular verb, "*Vayiḥan*" ("He" encamped at the mountain) to refer the Jewish nation. Normally, we would expect the Torah the plural form "*Vayaḥanu*," which would translate to "they encamped." Why does the Torah use the singular verb *Vayiḥan*?

This seemingly minor detail has amazing ramifications. Rashi[221] explains that this minor change signifies the unprecedented unity that the Jewish nation had at Har Sinai. Whenever the Jewish people arrived at a new location in any other place in the desert, there was always widespread disagreement and fighting amongst them. When they arrived at the foot of Har Sinai, however, they were united under a common cause to accept the Torah, "as one man and with one heart." Rashi highlights the crucial role of unity as a prerequisite to receiving the Torah.

This idea can also be seen in the Haggada of Pesaḥ. In the section of Dayyenu, the Haggada says: "*If Hashem had brought us before Har Sinai, but hadn't given us the Torah, it would have been enough for us to say thank you.*" [222] What does this passage mean? Wasn't the whole point of traveling to Har Sinai only for the Jews to receive the Torah? How can we say that it would have been enough to just go to Har Sinai, and not actually receive anything? The answer is that this passage underscores the monumental achievement of the unity that the Jewish people achieved at Har Sinai. This unity by itself was such a major accomplishment that even without the Torah, it would have been a reason for immense gratitude.

The importance of unity and love amongst the Jewish people cannot be overstated. The Gemara[223] teaches that the first Bet Hamikdash

---

221 Rashi Shemot 19:1-2, quoting Mechilta
222 Pesach Haggada, Maggid
223 Yoma 9b

(Temple) was destroyed because of the three cardinal sins: idol worship, forbidden relations, and bloodshed, each of which one is obligated to sacrifice their life for rather than commit. That generation unfortunately committed these capital transgressions and the first Bet Hamikdash was destroyed. However, during the second Temple period, the Jewish people were engaged in Torah study and observance of mitzvot. They did not commit the sinful acts that were performed in the First Temple period. So why was the second Bet Hamikdash destroyed? The Gemara explains that it was destroyed due to unprovoked hatred (*Sin'at Ḥinam*) during that period. This comes to teach us that the sin of unprovoked hatred is equivalent to the three severe transgressions: idol worship, prohibited relations and bloodshed (murder).[224]

The sin of *Sin'at Ḥinam*, unprovoked hatred, carries immense weight. As we approach the holiday of Shavuot, let us all strive to treat every Jew with love, respect, and understanding. With the help of Hashem, this should lead to more unity and togetherness in Am Yisrael, so that we can all deserve the ongoing privilege of accepting the Torah. Ḥag Sameaḥ!

---

[224] Yoma 9b

207

Insights on the Weekly Parasha and Jewish Holidays

תשעה באב

Tisha Be'av

From Tragedy to Transformation: Overcoming Baseless Hatred

Tisha Be'av, the ninth day of the Hebrew month of Av, is a day of national mourning on the Jewish Calendar. Most notably, the day commemorates the destruction of the first and second Bet Hamikdash in Yerushalayim, among other tragedies that occurred on this day. The Gemara[225] records the famous story of Kamtza and Bar Kamtza as an example of the cause of the downfall of the Bet Hamikdash. In this incident, a messenger was instructed to invite a friend, Kamtza, to the host's party. The messenger accidentally invited his enemy whose name was Bar Kamtza. Bar Kamtza innocently assumed that the host desired reconciliation and therefore invited him. When the host saw his enemy, Bar Kamtza, at the party, he publicly demanded that he leave the event. Bar Kamtza begged the host that he be allowed to stay to avoid humiliation, and eventually offered to pay for the whole party, but the host still refused and had him physically thrown out of the party. Bar Kamtza

---

[225] Gittin 55b

was so infuriated by the incident that he fabricated a false allegation against the Jews to the Roman emperor. Bar Kamtza's false allegation eventually led to the downfall and destruction of the Bet Hamikdash.

It is interesting to note that other historical records offer no mention of this specific incident or of a Bar Kamtza. If it was such a significant event that led to the destruction of Yerushalayim, why is there no mention of this episode? The answer to this may be the story of Kamtza and Bar Kamtza was not recorded to tell us about one specific incident that led to the destruction of the Bet Hamikdash. Rather, this incident was only one of the many examples of the widespread baseless hatred in Yerushalayim at that time. The story of Kamtza and Bar Kamtza is only one example that highlights an unfortunate general trend that was so rampant at the time. The principle that the Gemara is trying to teach us is that baseless hatred, such as the baseless hatred in this story, was what single-handedly brought the destruction of the Temple.

The Gemara[226] teaches us: The first Temple was destroyed because of the three cardinal sins - immorality, murder, and idol worship, while the second Temple was destroyed due to baseless hatred. It was this overarching attitude that destroyed everything we had. Unfortunately, this phenomenon has not yet been corrected and is still relevant nowadays. The internal conflict caused by baseless hatred is our own downfall. The pettiest of conflicts can cause marriages, families, and communities to fall apart.

It is crucial for us as a nation to learn how to coexist peacefully. We must learn to sometimes forego our differences and our egos to maintain harmony for the greater good. Promoting peace and harmony will allow us to live happier lives, by allowing us to let go

---

[226] Yoma 9b

of the pain and negative feelings in our hearts. By embracing these lessons, we contribute to building a world filled with peace. Only this can ultimately lead the coming of Mashiaḥ and the rebuilding of the Third Temple, speedily in our days, Amen.

Made in the USA
Columbia, SC
09 October 2024

329e3e99-fe74-4337-82b4-bd81c3e1d376R01